Touring China Eighty Years Ago

CHRONICLES FROM *NATIONAL GEOGRAPHIC*

Cultural and Geographical Exploration

Ancient Civilizations of the Aztecs and Maya

The Ancient Incas

Australia: The Unique Continent

Building the Panama Canal

Grand Canyon Experiences

Hawaii and the Islands of the Pacific:
A Visit to the South Seas

Indian Tribes of the Americas

Jerusalem and the Holy Land

Lighthouses: Beacons of the Sea

Mysteries of the Sahara

Race for the South Pole—The Antarctic Challenge

Rediscovering Ancient Egypt

Robert E. Peary and the Rush to the North Pole

The Russian People in 1914

Touring America Seventy-Five Years Ago

Touring China Eighty Years Ago

Touring China Eighty Years Ago

CHRONICLES FROM *NATIONAL GEOGRAPHIC*

Arthur M. Schlesinger, jr.
Senior Consulting Editor

Fred L. Israel
General Editor

Landstown High School
Media Center

CHELSEA HOUSE PUBLISHERS

Philadelphia

CHELSEA HOUSE PUBLISHERS

Editor in Chief Stephen Reginald
Managing Editor James D. Gallagher
Production Manager Pamela Loos
Art Director Sara Davis
Director of Photography Judy L. Hasday
Senior Production Editor LeeAnne Gelletly

The Chelsea House World Wide Web site address is
http://www.chelseahouse.com

First Printing

1 3 5 7 9 8 6 4 2

Library of Congress Cataloging-in-Publication Data

Muller, James Arthur, 1884–1945
Touring China eighty years ago: chronicles from National geographic /
Arthur M. Schlesinger, Jr., senior consulting editor: Fred L. Israel,
general editor.
    p. cm. — (Cultural and geographical exploration)
    "By James Arthur Muller" — P. 1.
    Includes index.
    Summary: Articles from issues of "National Geographic" magazine
    describe life in China during the first part of the twentieth century.
    ISBN 0-7910-5448-9
    1. China—Description and travel Juvenile literature. [1. China—Description
    and travel.] I. Schlesinger, Arthur Meier, 1917– . II. Israel, Fred L.
    III. Title. IV. Series.
    DS710.M75   1999
    951—dc21   99-41845
                           CIP

CONTENTS

"THE GREATEST EDUCATIONAL JOURNAL"

When the first *National Geographic* magazine appeared in October 1888, the United States totaled 38 states. Grover Cleveland was President. The nation's population hovered around 60 million. Great Britain's Queen Victoria also ruled as the Empress of India. William II became Kaiser of Germany that year. Czar Alexander III ruled Russia, and the Turkish Empire stretched from the Balkans to the tip of Arabia. To Westerners, the Far East was still a remote and mysterious land. Throughout the world, riding the back of an animal was the principal means of transportation. Unexplored and unmarked places dotted the global map.

On January 13, 1888, thirty-three men—scientists, cartographers, inventors, scholars, and explorers—met in Washington, D.C. They had accepted an invitation from Gardiner Greene Hubbard (1822–1897), the first president of the Bell Telephone Company and a leader in the education of the deaf, to form the National Geographic Society "to increase and diffuse geographic knowledge." One of the assembled group noted that they were the "first explorers of the Grand Canyon and the Yellowstone, those who had carried the American flag farthest north, who had measured the altitude of our famous mountains, traced the windings of our coasts and rivers, determined the distribution of flora and fauna, enlightened us in the customs of the aborigines, and marked out the path of storm and flood." Nine months later, the first issue of *National Geographic* magazine was sent out to 165 charter members. Today, more than a century later, membership has grown to an astounding 11 million in more than 170 nations. Several times that number regularly read the monthly issues of the *National Geographic* magazine.

The first years were difficult ones for the new magazine. The earliest volumes seem dreadfully scientific and quite dull. The articles in Volume I, No. 1 set the tone—W. M. Davis, "Geographic Methods in Geologic Investigation," followed by W. J. McGee, "The Classification of Geographic Forms by Genesis." Issues came out erratically—three in 1889, five in 1890, four in 1891; and two in 1895. In January 1896 "an illustrated monthly" was added to the title. The November issue that year contained a photograph of a half-naked Zulu bride and bridegroom in their wedding finery staring full face into the camera. But, a reader must have wondered what to make of the accompanying text: "These people . . . possess some excellent traits, but are horribly cruel when once they have smelled blood." In hopes of expanding circulation, the Board of Managers offered newsstand copies at $.25 each and began to accept advertising. But the magazine essentially remained unchanged. Circulation rose only slightly.

In January 1898, shortly after Gardiner Greene Hubbard's death, his son-in-law Alexander Graham Bell (1847–1922) agreed to succeed him as the second president of the National Geographic Society. Bell invented the telephone in 1876 and, while pursuing his lifelong goal of improving the lot of the deaf, had turned his amazingly versatile mind to contemplating such varied problems as human flight, air conditioning, and popularizing geography. The society then had about 1,100 members—the magazine was on the edge of bankruptcy. Bell did not want the job. He wrote in his diary, though, that he accepted leadership of the society "in order to save it." "Geography is a fascinating subject and it can be made interesting," he told the board of directors. Bell abandoned the unsuccessful attempt to increase circulation through newsstand sales. "Our journal," he wrote, "should go to members, people who believe in our work and want to help." He understood that the lure for prospective members should be an association with a society that made it possible for the average person to share with kings and scientists the excitement of sending an expedition to a strange land or an explorer to an inaccessible region. This idea, more than any other, has been responsible for the growth of the National Geographic Society and for the popularity of the magazine. "I can well remember," recalled Bell in 1912, "how the idea was laughed at that we should ever reach a membership of ten thousand." That year it had soared to 107,000!

Bell attributed this phenomenal growth, though, to one man who had transformed the *National Geographic* magazine into "the greatest educational journal in the world"—Gilbert H. Grosvenor (1875–1966). Bell had hired Grosvenor, then 24, in 1899 as the National Geographic Society's first full-time employee, "to put some life into the magazine." He personally escorted the new editor, who would become his son-in-law, to the society's headquarters—a small rented room shared with the American Forestry Association on the fifth floor of a building near the U.S. Treasury in downtown Washington. Grosvenor remembered the headquarters "littered with old magazines, newspapers, and a few record books and six enormous boxes crammed with *Geographics* returned by the newsstands." "No desk!" exclaimed Bell. "I'll send you mine." That afternoon, delivery men brought Grosvenor a large walnut rolltop and the new editor began to implement Bell's instructions—to transform the magazine from one of cold geographic fact "expressed in hieroglyphic terms which the layman could not understand into a vehicle for carrying the living, breathing, human-interest truth about this great world of ours to the people." And what did Bell consider appropriate "geographic subjects"? He replied: "The world and all that is in it is our theme."

Grosvenor shared Bell's vision of a great society and magazine that would disseminate geographic knowledge. "I thought of geography in terms of its Greek root: *geographia*—a description of the world," he later wrote. "It thus becomes the most catholic of subjects, universal in appeal, and embracing nations, people, plants, birds, fish. We would never lack interesting subjects." To attract readers, Grosvenor had to change the public attitude toward geography, which he knew was regarded as "one of the dullest of all subjects, something to inflict upon schoolboys and avoid in later life." He wondered why certain books that relied heavily on geographic description remained popular—Charles Darwin's *Voyage of the Beagle*, Richard Dana Jr.'s *Two Years Before the Mast*, and even Herodotus's *History*. Why did readers for generations—and with Herodotus's travels, for 20 centuries—return to these books? What did these volumes, which used so many geographic descriptions, have in common? What was the secret? According to Grosvenor, the answer was that "each was an accurate, eyewitness, firsthand account. Each contained simple straightforward writing—writing that sought to make pictures in the reader's mind."

Gilbert Grosvenor was editor of the *National Geographic* magazine for 55 years, from 1899 until 1954. Each of the 660 issues under his direction had been a highly readable geography textbook. He took Bell's vision and made it a reality. Acclaimed as "Mr. Geography," he discovered the earth anew for himself and for millions around the globe. He charted the dynamic course that the National Geographic Society and its magazine followed for more than half a century. In so doing, he forged an instrument for world education and understanding unique in this or any age. Under his direction, the *National Geographic* magazine grew in circulation from a few hundred copies—he recalled carrying them to the post office on his back—to more than five million at the time of his retirement as editor, enough for a stack 25 miles high.

This Chelsea House series celebrates Grosvenor's first 25 years as editor of the *National Geographic*. "The mind must see before it can believe," said Grosvenor. From the earliest days, he filled the magazine with photographs and established another Geographic principle—to portray people in their natural attire or lack of it. Within his own editorial committee, young Grosvenor encountered the prejudice that photographs had to be "scientific." Too often, this meant dullness. To Grosvenor, every picture and sentence had to be interesting to the layperson. "How could you educate and inform if you lost your audience by boring your readers?" Grosvenor would ask his staff. He persisted and succeeded in making the *National Geographic* magazine reflect this fascinating world.

To the young-in-heart of every age there is magic in the name *National Geographic*. The very words conjure up enchanting images of faraway places, explorers and scientists, sparkling seas and dazzling mountain peaks, strange plants, animals, people, and customs. The small society founded in 1888 "for the increase and diffusion of geographic knowledge" grew, under the guidance of one man, to become a great force for knowledge and understanding. This achievement lies in the genius of Gilbert H. Grosvenor, the architect and master builder of the National Geographic Society and its magazine.

Fred L. Israel
The City College of the City University of New York

TOURING CHINA EIGHTY YEARS AGO

Fred L. Israel

During the past one-hundred years, the *National Geographic* magazine has published more than 200 articles about China. These stories have dealt with the people of China, their way of life, and their physical surroundings. Together, these many articles have provided readers with an impressive mosaic of the Chinese civilization.

The five articles chosen for this compilation, written eighty years ago, attempt to explain the Chinese people and their culture at that time. The text and photographs reflect a convulsive political era—the years between the collapse of the Manchu dynasty and the struggle for a republican form of government, roughly the years 1911–23.

A vast country, China covers more than one-fifth of Asia. Only Russia and Canada can claim more territory. China's land area includes some of the world's driest deserts and highest mountains, as well as the world's richest farmland. The Chinese people take great pride in their land, as well as in their history and in their achievements.

Some of the greatest engineering works in history were completed by the Chinese. They built walls, roads, and canals, as well as magnificient imperial palaces and tombs. They constructed massive irrigation projects to bring water to the land, as well as drainage systems to prevent flooding. In China, the main rivers flow from east to west; canals were built to link these rivers by inland routes.

It had long been a Chinese practice to build protective walls around towns. From about the middle of the fourth century B.C., very long walls were constructed as barriers dividing the various Chinese autonomous states and separating these states from the so-called barbarian regions. When China unified at the end of the third century B.C., the emperor joined and extended the existing walls on the northern frontier, thus completing in 214 B.C. the first Great Wall. It was built for defense as China has no natural barriers along its northern border to stop invaders. Obviously, the invention of gun powder would eventually make this structure obsolete.

Nevertheless, the Great Wall is overwhelming. It is one of the largest construction projects ever carried out. With all its branches, it runs about 4,000 miles between the east coast and north-central China. The Great Wall winds over mountains and through forests, valleys, and deserts. It is made of earth and gravel and, since the 14th century, most of it has been faced with brick. Erected entirely by the hands of more than 300,000 forced laborers conscripted from all over China, the wall stands as the longest structure in the world and the only man-made object astronauts were able to see on earth while circling the moon.

The highest sections of the Great Wall are near Beijing, where it is 35-feet high and about 25-feet wide at its base. Watchtowers stand every 100 to 200 yards. About 40-feet high, the towers once served as lookout posts. Although most of the Great Wall is in ruins today, records inform us that the army cavalry riding horse-drawn chariots could race five abreast from post to post along its top.

Today, many more people in the world consider themselves Chinese than there are residents of Europe and North America combined. The society and culture of this complex civilization is truly extraordinary. In each period of their history, the Chinese have made use of what they inherited but also have devised new concepts. The articles in this book try to render intelligible for Westerners the great Chinese character that has survived through the centuries; these stories help us to better understand the Chinese people—their history and their artifacts.

PEKING, THE CITY OF THE UNEXPECTED

By James Arthur Muller

AS ONE passes within the walls of Peking he expects to find, as in other Chinese cities, the bannered signs of shopkeepers throwing gay canopies across narrow, tortuous, huddled streets; but behold! broad avenues three miles long, crossed by other broad avenues three miles long, making squares as regular as those of a checkerboard.

The visitor wonders whether the builders of this city saw in prophetic vision the streets of Chicago, Denver, and Philadelphia. Then he begins to suspect that Peking is the one spacious Chinese city because it is not a Chinese city at all, but a Tatar city, built by adventurous barbarians of the north, men who lived in the saddle, upon steppes and plains, whose feet were set in a large room.

THE CAMELS AND CARTS OF PEKING

Wonder does not stop with the length, breadth, and regularity of the streets. The traffic upon them is equally unexpected. In the cities of southern China sedan-chairs edge their way with difficulty through the crowds of pedestrians and carrying coolies, who jostle each other in the narrow lanes. In Peking every street is alive with beasts and vehicles.

Down the smooth, tree-lined, macadam center-roads autos, cabs, rickshaws, and bicycles speed past slow-moving catafalques and crimson wedding processions. On each side, between sidewalk and trees, along a highway of turf, go mule-mounted equestrians, soldiers on sturdy Manchurian ponies, triplets of donkeys hauling lumber, brick, coal, and crockery, portly old gentlemen straddling diminutive asses, blue-canopied Peking carts, and caravans of camels out of the north.

Imagine a city where camels go up and down the streets upon legitimate business, not in a circus parade! The visitor strolls along Hatamen Street after breakfast, and there they are, on their knees, blinking in the morning sun—fine, shaggy, brown beasts, an occasional white one—rather dirty white—among them, chewing their cuds in leisure. The pavement before the shops whither they have carried merchandise has been their caravansary for the night. There are dozens upon dozens of them lining the sidewalk, up the street and down.

INSTEAD OF NARROW, TORTUOUS STREETS, PEKING HAS STRAIGHT, BROAD THOROUGHFARES, MANY OF THEM THREE MILES LONG

The explanation for the difference in physical aspect between China's capital and such cities as Shanghai, Canton, and Hankow is that Peking is a Tatar rather than a Chinese city, for it was built by adventurous barbarians of the north, men who lived in the saddle and upon the steppes and plains (see text, page 1).

THE GATE TO THE IMPERIAL CITY PEKING

Occupying the center of the Inner (Tatar) City, the Imperial City is inclosed by a rectangular brick wall. In the center of this city is the Purple Forbidden Palace, within which, in turn, was the Emperor's Palace, containing many halls of vast proportions, magnificently decorated.

By and by the drivers come forth, throw their empty sacks between the humps of the animals, rouse them, and lead them off down the street, slowly and softly stepping, in single file, out beneath the great stone arches of the Hata Gate, then westward beside the frowning buttresses of the city wall.

Almost as fascinating as the camels are the carts of Peking, or rather the little beasts which pull them—ponies, donkeys, mules, and non-descript, elusive creatures that are neither horse, mule, nor ass, but subtle, indistinguishable mixtures. On first sight one is sure they are horses, on the second he is sure they are mules, on the third he is equally sure they are zebras with the stripes worn off. One historian of China speaks of the ancient Tatars as possessing horses, asses, mules, and "other peculiar breeds of the equine family." These ancient other breeds still trot about the Tatar city.

ON THE WIDE NEW STREETS OF PEKING,
WITH A GATEWAY IN THE BACKGROUND

The many gates of the city are closed from sundown to sunrise, and nothing short of a governor's edict will enable one to get in or out during those hours. Note the popularity of the wheeled vehicle.

A CITY WITHOUT A SKYLINE

If streets and traffic, carts and camels are unexpected, no less so are the buildings. The traveler who has seen pictures of the majestic temples and palaces of Peking enters the imposing South Gate prepared for architectural raptures. But he finds the broad, straight highways of the city lined with insignificant one-story shops or with equally insignificant gray, windowless, one-story house walls, or long, unlovely, stretches of dull red plastered fence walls.

One writer discovered that the beauty of Fifth Avenue lay in its skyline of magnificent cornices. The streets of Peking have neither skyline nor cornices. Were it not for the multitudinous trafffic upon them, they would remind the traveler of the sprawling, God-forsaken streets of an American mining town, infinitely extended. The trees which line the central roadways are all of such recent planting that this city of the centuries suggests the latest offspring of an energetic real-estate agent.

BUILDINGS THAT SHOUT WITH BARBARIC COLOR

As soon, however, as the traveler enters a gateway, through one of the gray or dingy brick-red walls, he comes suddenly and unexpectedly upon a palace, silent in the sun, yet shouting aloud in the barbaric brilliance of its color—crimson columns, friezes of flashing gold on green, wide-flaring roofs of resplendent yellow, all above a triple-terraced platform of marble, white like snow. Or it may be a many-courted temple, where a hundred lamas drone chants before an inscrutable Buddha; or a wooded park, where emperors once took their pleasure, where

PEKING SHOPS ARE NOTED FOR THEIR CONTENTS
RATHER THAN FOR THEIR ARCHITECTURAL EXTERIORS

The broad, straight highways are lined with insignificant one-story buildings and gray, windowless houses, with here and there a stretch of dull-red, plastered fence wall.

century-old cedars shade pathways and pleasant lakes. Shrines nestle in mulberry groves and hillocks are crowned by Buddhist topes, from whose marble bases one looks out over the roofs of the city—miles and miles, it seems, of gray roofs—and in the center of all a great splotch of imperial yellow, the once "forbidden city," where dwelt the emperor, his sons and his daughters, his wives and his concubines.

Even the foreigners in Peking have fallen into this habit of surrounding themselves with blank and unexpressive walls; so that behind such barriers are found not only temples and parks, and palaces, but colleges and churches and legation buildings.

THE UNEXPECTED IS THE KEYNOTE OF CHINESE ARCHITECTURE

Indeed, the unexpected is the essence of Chinese architecture. One can never get a complete view of a temple or a yamen unless

A CAMEL CARAVAN ARRIVING IN PEKING

Mule-mounted equestrians; soldiers on sturdy Manchurian ponies; portly old gentlemen astride diminutive assess; autos, cabs, rickshaws, bicycles, and caravans of camels out of the north—all go up and down the streets of Peking on legitimate business, not in a circus parade!

there be some adjacent hill or tower or city wall from which to view it.

On level ground only the outer wall and the entrance are seen, and when these are passed one sees only the first court, with its more elaborate entrance to the second; and so on through three, four, five, six, it may be seven, courtyards, each complete in itself, each with a central building, through which one passes to the court beyond, each building larger, higher, or more decorative than the last, each breaking upon the beholder with a fresh surprise.

This arrangement, admirable as it is in producing sudden and increasing wonder and in allowing the architect to work up to a climax through a series of surprising effects, fails at times in its lack of vista. This is notably true of smaller buildings, which sometimes appear cramped and huddled, sometimes cosy and pleasing, seldom imposing. But in Peking, where Chinese building has reached its most magnificent development, there is a fine spaciousness in the courtyards, so combined with massive structure, restraint, and dignity of line and simple coloring that one fairly catches his breath in admiration at the strength and power of it.

This is especially true of the imperial palace, which is perhaps the most effectively arranged group of buildings in all China. Gateway after gateway, each gate a palace in itself, pillared, roofed, and buttressed, leads into a wide-lying courtyard whose placid expanse dwarfs ancient trees around its edges into seeming shrubs.

Each court is a unit of grandeur and magnificence in itself, and at the same time an integral member of a series leading up to the marble-terraced courtyard of the great throne hall.

Although the imperial palace is the finest architectural ensemble in the capital, in the Temple of Heaven, or, as the Chinese call it, "The Happy Year Hall," it is where the emperor used to offer annual supplication to Heaven for a prosperous new year, that we find a single building in which the simple dignity of Chinese architecture is at its best.

This is perhaps the most frequently pictured of all Chinese buildings. Every Chinese photographer displays it in his window; every vender of post-cards features it; every book on China reproduces it; it is probably the one view of things Chinese which every Westerner who knows anything at all about China has seen. Yet I know of no building which most pictures fail so pitifully to portray.

In the usual print or photograph it is squat, plump, and heavy, like a German wedding cake. In reality it is strong and gracious and mighty, and when the visitor comes into its presence he has come into the presence of a great peace.

There it stands on a vast platform, its base above the tree-tops. Above the platform is a threefold marble terrace, white and circular; then red columns green-gold friezes, and three fine, flaring, circular roofs, with shadows and mystery under the eaves, and the roof tiles not crying-yellow, like those of the imperial palace, but deep, deep blue.

It is the "quietness and confidence" of which Isaiah speaks, made visible in wood and tile and marble.

THE ELEMENT OF SURPRISE LEADS CHINESE ARCHITECTURE ASTRAY

But it is just in this, its chief masterpiece, that Chinese architecture, in its insistence on the unexpected, has gone farthest astray. The temple is in the midst of a huge park; acres of lawn and dense groves of ancient evergreen surround it; there is every condition conducive to the most effective use of distance and vista, yet the temple approaches are so clouded and cluttered with cheap, tawdry, decadent gateways that nothing of the temple itself is seen until one actually stumbles upon it through the last gate.

The spirit of the building demands that the beholder draw near gradually and with reverence, not pop upon it like a jack out of the box.

THE DRAGON SCREEN A MARVEL OF PICTORIAL ART

Another of the unexpected treasures of Peking is the dragon screen. It is barely mentioned in some of the guidebooks and not mentioned at all in others. It is hidden behind a hillock in the winter palace grounds, and nine-tenths of the visitors to Peking walk within a hundred yards of it and never dream of its existence.

It is a wall perhaps twenty feet high and a hundred long, faced completely with tile cast to represent nine life-size dragons in bas-relief, of various colors—yellow, purple, buff, maroon, orange—dancing gaily above emerald billows, against a pale-blue sky.

Doubtless one should not speak of "life-size" dragons; but these creatures of the screen

CAMELS CEASE TO BE POETIC "SHIPS OF THE DESERT" IN PEKING:
THEY ARE COMMONPLACE BEASTS OF BURDEN

They are fine, shaggy, brown beasts, with an occasional white one—rather dirty white. Usually their caravansary for the night is the pavement in front of the shop at which they deliver their merchandise.

"OTHER PECULIAR BREEDS OF THE EQUINE FAMILY"

Thus speaks a historian of the Tatars in describing those "elusive little creatures of Peking which are neither horse, mule, nor ass, but subtle, indistinguishable mixtures" (see text, page 3).

THE BURDEN FREQUENTLY SEEMS OUT OF
ALL PROPORTION TO THE SIZE OF THE BEARER

Along Peking's highways of turf go triplets of donkeys hauling timber, brick, coal, and crockery. Note the rope traces by which two animals are harnessed in front of the beast next to the cart.

ALMOST AS FASCINATING AS ITS CAMELS AND DONKEYS ARE THE CARTS OF PEKING

Another type of two-wheeled vehicle commonly seen in the streets of China's capital is shown. Before the introduction of the rickshaw, these were the only vehicles of Peking.

CAMEL-BACK BRIDGE IN THE GROUNDS OF THE IMPERIAL SUMMER PALACE
Note the elaborately carved white marble railings.

are the alivest dragons one may ever hope to see; they give rise to the feeling that if a dragon lived he would be exactly like one of these.

Most sculptured Chinese dragons are life-less, angular beasts; but here there is an almost un-Chinese vigor and audacity in the spring and twist of the the lithe bodies. They leap, whirl, lunge, and writhe until the spectator steps back, half afraid that they will come tum-bling off the screen, striking at the unwary with their sturdy claws. There are, I believe, critics who teach that plastic art should never under-take to portray moments of activity. If this be correct, the dragons stand condemned; but if the sculptor may ever rightly give us life in its vivid, moving moments, here is a masterpiece.

THE WOMEN OF PEKING
A SOURCE OF SURPRISE

Dragons and donkeys, fanes and thor-oughfares, caravans and castles, do not exhaust the list of things unexpected which await the traveler in Peking. There also are the people.

The first strikingly surprising custom among them is that the women wear skirts. To a traveler fresh from America this would seem as it should be, but to one resident in the land of trousered women it appears almost immodest!

They not only wear skirts; they further approximate Western usage by painting their faces. Broadway is nature itself in comparison; for in Peking there are no light, artistic touch-

THE PORCELAIN PAGODA,
NEAR THE SUMMER PALACE

Most Chinese pagodas are built of brick, while similar structures in Japan, because of the frequency of
earthquakes, are built of wood.

es, but bold cheek circles of red upon frankly whitened faces—cosmetics unabashed.

These are the Manchu women. The Manchu men, descendants of the roving Tatars, go futilely about this spacious city of their fathers balancing trick birds upon their wrists; for, now that the empire is no more, their only occupation, that of ruling it, is gone, and the conquered Chinese, immemorial city-dwellers, are masters of the capital. It is a significant illustration of the age-old ability of the Chinese to absorb and enervate their conquerors.

A CITY OF HOPES AS WELL AS OF SPLENDID MEMORIES

It is not only at the Manchu dwellers of Peking that the visitor is surprised. There is that among the Chinese which is equally a cause for astonishment; for, although Peking is the recognized center of the reactionary North, it is none the less the center of the New China.

One who is familiar with Chinese political and social conditions expects to find Peking corrupt and contented; nor is he disappointed. In the palaces, the government offices and the multitude of barracks which surround the city, some self-seeking gangs of grafters who have plundered the Chinese people since the overthrow of the monarchy are still to be found. But the age-long Chinese tradition which would have centers of government also centers of learning has, in spite of reactionary rulers, filled the capital with thousands of eager students, for whom Peking is not only a city of splendid memories, but a city of hopes.

There is the Peking University, a first-class American mission institution; the University of Peking, an equally high-grade government school; the new Chin Hwa College and a score or more of other schools.

ASTRONOMICAL INSTRUMENTS IN THE OLDEST OBSERVATORY IN THE WORLD, FOUNDED BY KUBLAI KHAN, AT PEKING, IN THE THIRTEENTH CENTURY

Most of the bronze instruments of today were made by the Jesuit priest Verbiest from the original Chinese models. When Peking was looted in 1900, some of the finest of these instruments were seized by the Germans and sent to the imperial gardens at Potsdam. By a provision of the Treaty of Versailles, Germany undertook "to restore to China, within twelve months from the coming into force of the present treaty, all the astronomical instruments which her troops in 1900-1901 carried away from China, and to defray all expenses which may be incurred in effecting such restoration, including the expenses of dismounting, packing, transporting, insurance, and installation in Peking."

A MARVEL OF PICTORIAL ART, A SECTION OF PEKING'S DRAGON SCREEN

These horrendous creatures in bas-relief tile-work of various colors—yellow, purple, buff, maroon, and orange—dance gaily above emerald billows against a pale-blue sky. The screen is 20 feet high and 100 feet long (see text, page 7).

It was among the students and teachers of Peking, particularly among those of the universities, that the recent liberal movement in China started, and continued in the face of wholesale arrests and suppression by corrupt officials. By the Peking students the movement has been spread throughout the land, until now, for the first time in Chinese history, there is a really united national public opinion, directed not only against foreign aggression, but against Chinese governmental peculation as well.

To find Peking the source and center of this forward-looking movement for reform is not the least of the surprises which await the visitor to the capital.

Indeed, to most Western visitors the most unexpected thing of all is to find that the real China, the China which holds, potentially, the future of the Orient in her hands, is to be found in these colleges and in the technical schools and hospitals and churches, which look so like churches and hospitals and technical schools at home that the tourist ofttimes fails utterly to see them or their significance in his search for the romance and glamor of antiquity.

LAMA TEMPLE ADJOINS THAT OF CONFUCIUS

The tourist is not to be blamed for his blindness, however. He can see colleges, churches, and hospitals a plenty in the West; but a Lama temple, or a Confucian hall of classics, or a Taoist shrine is not to be come upon in Boston or Milwaukee. In the abundance of these relics of a passing age Peking, above all Chinese cities, is the queen.

THE ALTAR OF HEAVEN OF THE TEMPLE OF HEAVEN: PEKING

Arranged in three terraces of white marble, the altar is reached by 27 steps in three flights of nine steps each (see text, page 7). The whole plan is developed with mathematical exactness and with reference to lucky numbers. Here, before the days of the Republic, the Emperor used to prostrate himself annually. On the occasion of this ceremony he was accompanied by thousands of officials, all gorgeously gowned.

In the great Lama temple in the northwest corner of the city, with its seven sun-lit court-yards and its hundred deities, one may see on any forenoon threescore yellow-coated novices droning the morning lesson, cross-legged, before the many-handed God of Mercy, or half a dozen monks in purple palliums celebrating a Lamist mass with rice out of a silver bowl and wine from a gold-mounted chalice fashioned from a human skull.

The smoke of incense fills the nostrils of the placid Buddhas who sit above the high altar; countless little cup-shaped butter lamps are lighted, and to the accompaniment of drum, gong, and cymbal the monotone of the celebrant rises to a wild chant.

Just across the street from these idolatrous lamas, who represent the Buddhism of Tibet and who minister chiefly to the Mongols of the North, is the quiet, shady close of the temple of Confucius, wherein are neither monks nor idols.

Here the master is represented by a simple wooden tablet bearing the letters of his name. It is but little more exalted than the tablets of the four notable philosophers and the twelve particular disciples who share the hall with him, and the two and seventy famous scholars whose names are recorded in the long, low building on the sides of the court.

To this memorial to China's men of learning come educators and officials at the spring and autumn equinox to offer sacrifice. The ceremony, say many Confucianists, is not one of worship, but rather of grateful remembrance of the author of learning and his distinguished followers, whose moral maxims have been at the basis of China's life for almost three millenniums.

THE GAY THRONGS
AT A NEW YEAR FAIR

While the Lama temple stands for the decadent worship of Mongols and Manchus and the Confucian temple for the cult of Chinese scholars, it is in the Taoist temples that one finds the traditions of folk superstition still alive.

Here firecrackers are lighted before the God of Valor, paper ingots of gold burnt before the God of Wealth, and joss-sticks offered to the Guardian of the Eastern Mountain. Here, also, at the New Year season, are the fairs and, if the temple grounds be large enough, the horse-races.

Enterprising restaurateurs set up matting booths along the course, where the holiday-makers sip tea and munch peanuts and bread while they watch the men of the North ride furiously by on slender mules or stocky Manchurian ponies.

Meanwhile the temple courts are filled with mountebanks, jugglers, magicians, venders of figs, cigarettes, and candied rice balls, and sellers of fans, ribbons, mirrors, and tinsel jewelry, proprietors of peep-shows, and professional storytellers, like medieval troubadours, who gather a crowd to hear an old romance, half told, half chanted, to the sporadic accompaniment of drum or cymbal. In the midst of an exciting episode these storytellers pause and politely inform their auditors that the tale will be continued after another collection!

It is likewise to the temple courts that merchants on bazaar days bring their wares—wares not only to catch the pennies of the populace, but also the dollars of the tourist: vases of cloisonné, beads of amber, bottles of jade, lanterns of silk painted daintily with gold fish and lotus flowers, bronzes, none of which, you are solemnly assured, is later than the thirteenth century, and embroideries into which the souls of countless nameless artists have been stitched.

Sinuous dragons of gold, peach blossoms of pink, butterflies of every hue, are wrought upon silks of blue, green, and crimson.

Now that China has adopted gray republican simplicity, Mandarin coats, court dresses, whole wardrobes of impecunious Manchus, have found their way into the hands of the dealers. Here are opera cloaks for milady, and gay handbags and pillow-covers; for the cunning dealers have learned the taste of the West and have converted sleeve bands into table-runners and skirts into piano scarfs.

Far less costly, but no less significant to one who would interpret the life of the Orient, are the toys; for toys are the symbols and sacraments of the unity of mankind. It would be impossible for one to walk through the bazaars of Peking and not discover that the children of China are just like children the world over. Toys of the same sort delight them all. Here are flutes and drums, tops and diabolos, diminutive sets of furniture and dishes for a household of dolls, jointed bamboo dragons wriggling on a stick, tufted camels and gaudy tigers of painted canvas stuffed with sawdust, and little fuzzy dogs, of the Peking variety, which bark huskily when you squeeze their stomachs.

A MODERN CHINESE WOMAN
AN IDEAL HOSTESS

If the children of China are like the children of the West, the grown-ups cannot be quite so different, as we sometimes imagine. Indeed, in this city of antiquity one stumbles upon bits of the most extraordinary social modernity.

My host took me to call one afternoon at the home of a noted Chinese physician. He was away at the time, in the interest of the anti-opium movement, so his wife received us.

For a Chinese woman to receive two gentlemen in the absence of her husband is in itself something extraordinary. It is considered very modern for a Chinese wife even to be present when her husband receives guests; but Mrs. Tsen acted the hostess as graciously and as deftly as the most socially experienced hostess of the West. She poured tea, and when the conservation turned to Chinese music she went to the piano and showed how an ancient Chinese melody could be expressed in Western

THE SUMMER PALACE, ON THE SLOPE OF
THE MOUNTAIN OF TEN THOUSAND ANCIENTS

"The stately pleasure dome of the poet's imaginings, with its graceful, spiry, triple-roofed pavilion set upon a massive four-square base of stone, towering above porticos and pailous, summer-houses, grottos, islands, lily ponds, and bridges of marble" (see text, page 18).

notation; then she sang it for us, without the least embarrassment.

She told how her home had become the gathering place for the younger Chinese in the professions in Peking, especially those who had returned from study abroad. Then she pointed to the phonograph in the corner. "Oh! yes," she exclaimed, "of course I dance; we frequently have phonograph dances for our young Chinese friends."

I had to pinch myself to be sure that I was in China, in a Chinese home, talking to a Chinese woman, in the heart of the conservative North. Phonograph dances within four hours of the Great Wall! After this nothing in Peking was unexpected.

AMONG THE BEAUTIFUL
HILLS TO THE WEST OF PEKING

The initial reaction of the visitor to much that he sees in Peking, as I have hinted, is apt to be one of disappointment, followed by surprise, then by delight and admiration.

When he leaves the city gates and goes to the western hills, there is surprise and delight, but no initial disappointment. Perhaps that is because he has heard so much of the city and so little of the hills that he goes expecting nothing; perhaps it is because the hills, in spite of their barrenness, are altogether lovely.

However that may be, half the charm of Peking is not in Peking at all, but in its sur-

THE MARBLE BOAT ON THE LAKE AT THE SUMMER PALACE, NEAR PEKING

"It was all so pleasant and sunny and spacious and peaceful, so like a garden in wonderland, that I could forgive even that most absurd of all architectural absurdities, the notorious marble boat, built by the late Empress Dowager as a pleasure-house."

roundings. Shrine upon shrine, palace upon palace, lie without the city walls. They dot the surrounding plain; they nest on near-by wooded knolls; they lodge in crevices of the wide-circling, treeless hills—those quiet hills, slow curving, like billows after storm; verdant and velvety in summer; in winter bare and red-brown, deepening into twilight purple.

My host knew well the charm of the hills; so when, in my first rash judgment on the city, I hinted that I found it dusty and sprawling and not as I expected, he took me off to the hills. That was before I had seen the blue peace of the Temple of Heaven, or the yellow splendor of the Forbidden City, or the many hues and the agility of the rampant dragons; for he knew

that, to understand Peking and to love it, one must feel its glory in the setting of the hills, not see it through the critical dust of the streeted plain.

So on the morning after my arrival we put ourselves into two rickshaws and our quilts and blankets into a third, for every provident traveler in China carries his bed with him, and away we went, three and a half miles, at a dog trot, to the western gate, thence seven more over the willow-shaded highway to the Mountain of Ten Thousand Ancients, a pleasant wooded hillock, deep green against the bare brown of the January hills.

Before it lies a broad lake and on its slope stands the far-famed Summer Palace. Though several centuries more recent than Kublai Khan, this is indeed the stately pleasure dome of the poet's imaginings. Kublai might well have decreed it, with its graceful, spiry, triple-roofed pavilion set upon a massive four-square base of stone, towering above porticos and pailous, kiosks and summer houses, grottos and labyrinthine passages, islands and lily ponds, bridges of marble, and grotesque dragons cast in bronze.

There was ice three feet thick on the lake where lotus flowers bloom in summer; but the sun shone gloriously, illumining golden roofs and deepening the foliage of pine and cedar, and on the hilltop behind and above the palace shone a temple all of glazed tile, mottled green and yellow, glowing like a jeweled crown.

The wintry weather, coupled with the one-dollar admission fee, gave us the whole vast inclosure to ourselves. Here I had my first opportunity in China to eat my lunch in the open unsurrounded by a concourse of the curious!

It was all so pleasant and sunny and spacious and peaceful, so like a garden in wonderland, that I could forgive even that most absurd of all architectural absurdities, the notorious marble boat, built by the late Empress Dowager as a pleasure-house upon the lake.

CLASSIC LEGEND OF
THE BEACON TOWERS

We took to our rickshaws again in the afternoon and away we trotted toward the hills for seven miles more, past the Jade Fountain Pagoda, past leisurely camel trains, beyond the high road and the dust of tourist autos, under the shadow of somber, square, beacon towers, marching in single file, at half-mile intervals, out over the hill crests.

The Chinese have a classic legend about these beacon towers. It is the Oriental counterpart of Æsop's "Wolf! Wolf!"

Once upon a time the emperor, so runs the story, was deeply in love with a melancholy beauty who would not smile. In vain he tried to banish her ennui until he hit upon the scheme of lighting the beacons.

Flames leaped up from tower after tower, rousing the country-side; the host assembled. Horsemen on shaggy ponies from the northern plains, crossbowmen in jointed bamboo armor, scimitared warriors with grim painted faces, poured into the capital.

The imperial lady was delighted with the pageant, and when she saw the disgust upon the faces of the clansmen as they learned they had been summoned to make a Dulcinea's holiday, she even smiled.

Not long after this the Tatars broke over the wall. Again the beacon towers lifted their fires against the hills; but no host responded. The city was taken, the emperor slain, and the melancholy beauty carried off by the wild men of the north.

IN THE TEMPLE OF
THE SLEEPING BUDDHA

We crossed the line of beacon towers, ran along a rough, pebbly lane to the foot of the brown hills; then up a short, broad avenue of ancient cedars, under a magnificent pailou of red, green, and yellow into the courtyard of the Sleeping Buddha.

There, in the central hall of worship, he reclines upon his elbow, a bronze figure twenty feet long, surrounded by pairs of huge cloth slippers, left as votive offerings by pious pilgrims to protect him, presumably, from unhallowed tacks, should he walk in his sleep.

THE GREAT WALL OF CHINA FROM A POINT TO THE EAST OF NANKOW PASS
"Away it goes, before and behind; up, up the topmost ridges of the hills—bending, swinging, climbing, leaping like the supple dragons of the palace-garden screen. It undulates, it sways, it marches before, it takes the curve of the hills like a swift auto on a mountain road."

It is this temple, or rather the temple inclosure beyond the main building, which the Princeton Center in Peking has leased as a vacation home. There are tennis courts, swimming pools, a modern kitchen and dining-room, and space for several score cot beds in buildings once devoted to monastic uses; but the bronze Buddha sleeps on, unmindful of these innovations, and a few monks still burn incense daily before him.

After supper with the Sleeping Buddha, we crawled into our blanket bags and tried to follow his somnolent example. Our bedroom was a sort of little summer building, with the front quite open, perched high upon a rock among the pine tops. It had been the shrine of Kwan Yin, Buddhist Goddess of Mercy, but when the Princetonians moved in, the monks deemed it no fit place for a goddess! She moved out and was buried by her servitors in the hillside, back of the shrine. So we lay in her place, the crisp winter air of the hills in our nostrils, a flood of moonlight in our eyes, making a gilded mystery of temple roofs and pine shadows, and in our ears and dreams the temple bells a-calling, for all night long the little brazen bells, which hang lightly from the overjetting corners of the roof, swayed and tingled drowsily in the wind.

Next morning the sun shone as it can only in the cold, dry winter of north China, like a brand-new sun, shining for the first time from a fleckless sky, blue above bright-brown hills. It must have been in such a sun that the Psalmist sang of the little hills that skipped like lambs and the mountains like young sheep. Even the barren hills of Peking are resilient in such sunshine.

Again we set out behind our indefatigable rickshaw men, first to Pi Yun Ssu, the Temple of the Green Jade Clouds, the loveliest temple in the north, a cube of pure white marble set in a grove of lustrous, white-stemmed pines.

Then we turned toward the city again by a route different from that by which we came. It took us past the Old Summer Palace, left a ruin by the Anglo-French punitive expedition of 1860. What was once an imperial residence of unprecedented extent and magnificence is now a place of heaps, with here and there a broken arch or a shattered pillar still standing, strangely reminiscent of France or Italy; for this palace, built in the eighteenth century, in the style of Versailles, was planned by Jesuit fathers, then in high favor at the imperial court.

It is one of the most unexpected of the unexpected things in Peking, to come suddenly upon a Renaissance portal or a cluster of Ionic columns among the ruins of a Chinese emperor's pleasure house.

HOW AMERICA'S BOXER INDEMNITY FUNDS WERE SPENT

Adjacent to these remains there stands, by a kind of historic compensation, Chin Hwa College, with most modern equipment—library, assembly hall, gymnasium, science buildings—built and maintained with that portion of the Boxer indemnity which the United States gave back to China. When one thinks of the incalculable repayment in international friendliness and the boundless admiration among the Chinese for the United States which has come from that small gift, one wonders why it is that nations have not more frequently dealt with one another in the same generous fashion.

A week later I went out again from the city, this time to the Great Wall. Now when I look back it seems like a dream. It is not quite believable that I have really been to the goal of my childhood's imaginings, that last fence of the universe, the Great Wall of China. More improbable still does it seem to have ridden to it and through it in a modern railroad train.

The world has surely grown small when travel agencies in Peking can advertise a day's excursion to the Great Wall.

It is wonder enough for one journey to have walked atop the wall and looked out over the dusty brown plains of the north where Tatar horsemen once swarmed toward the passes, and to have seen trains of pack-mules straggling through the great stone gateways, oblivious of the traffic on the near-by rails, their backs laden with merchandise as were the backs of pack-mules two thousand years ago.

THE SPELL OF THE GREAT WALL OF CHINA

Like so much in or near Peking, the Great Wall is at first disappointing. It is disappointingly small. It is, in places, only twenty feet high and as many broad, while the city wall of Peking is twice as high and, at the base, thrice as broad, with huge ten-storied watch-towers at each corner.

When one stands close under the Peking city wall it looms above with the massive grandeur of an abrupt high cliff; but when the traveler gets off the train at the Nankow Pass and sees the bit of wall scrambling up the hill-

A FLANKING TOWER ON THE BATTLEMENTED WALLS OF PEKING

The numerous window-like openings were designed for archers defending the city. Note the canopied Peking cart in the foreground.

side before him, he wonders why it is called "great."

That, however, is only at first. He has only to climb up out of the pass and follow the wall for half an hour and he begins to understand.

Away it goes before him, and behind, up, up the topmost ridges of the hills—bending, swinging, climbing, leaping like the supple, agile dragons of the palace-garden screen. It undulates, it sways, it marches before, it takes the curve of the hills like a swift auto on a mountain road, on and on and on, across the farthest gully, beyond the farthest peak. Where

the mountains blend into the clouds, there it is; where the last horizon vanishes, it is there.

One sits in the shadow of a watch-tower and through its windows gets arch-framed pictures of bulwarks and bastions and exultant curves; and he remembers that this wall was begun two hundred years before the birth of Christ, and was added to throughout the centuries, until it compassed fifteen hundred miles.

In places of strategic importance, as here at the Nankow Pass, there were once five giant loops, with miles of country between, so that if one were taken the next might be defended; and every hundred yards there is a watch-tower.

It is at once the most daring, the most colossal, the most graceful, architectural concept which the mind of ancient man was given to fulfill. The sheer audacity of the thing, especially in the light of China's unaudacious character today, is staggering.

THE DISMISSED RICKSHAW MAN AND HIS SMILE

By an ironic coincidence it was on the way to the Great Wall that I met the unaudacious rickshaw man. The first stage of our journey—from my host's rooms to the railroad station—was a distance of four miles. One of our rickshaw coolies was young and lusty and a good runner; the other was old—not very old in years, but old for a rickshaw man in a city where distances are long and legs and lungs must be in prime condition to suit impatient Americans.

The old man started off briskly enough, but we had hardly rounded the corner into the main street when it became clear that he could not stand the necessary pace for forty minutes.

"We must catch that train," said my host, "and this old chap won't get us there." So I hailed the first sturdy coolie I saw and stepped into his rickshaw.

"Give the old man four coppers," said my host.

I did so without further thought at the moment, saw the old fellow regard his younger rival with that resigned, pitiful smile with which the Chinese are wont to accept the inevitable, and we were off.

His smile haunted me. I began to feel that I had broken a contract with him; he had been engaged for a ride to the railroad at a fare of thirty coppers; he had been dismissed with four.

"Don't let that trouble you," said my host. "It is understood among rickshaw men that if they cannot pull at the speed you want, you are free to dismiss them. Four coppers are twice as much as he earned."

My host had had considerable experience with Peking rickshaw men. He was doubtless right. But all day long that half good-natured, half regretful, altogether pathetic smile of the old man was somehow mixed up with the glory of wind and sunshine on the brown hills and the wild leaping curves of the ramparts.

It is this unexpected smile at misfortune which makes life bearable for millions of Chinese. I wonder whether it is this same smile which makes progress in China so difficult? That is a problem I have not solved; but I have, ever since, paid riotous rickshaw fares in memory of the old fellow who took me four coppers' worth toward the Great Wall.

THE EDEN OF THE FLOWERY REPUBLIC

By Dr. Joseph Beech

A THOUSAND miles westward from the coast of China the Yangtze River, which in Chinese means "The Child of the Ocean," in its passage through the outer rim of central Asia's mountain system has carved, in surpassing beauty and majestic grandeur, the five gorges of the upper Yangtze, rightly called the gateways to West China. They stretch from Ichang, until recently the head of steam navigation, to Kweichow, a distance of 125 miles.

The traveler is prompted to call "Hats off!" as he sails between these massive walls, crowned with cathedral domes that companion with the clouds, and his admiration is mingled with awe of the river, with its succession of rapids and treacherous whirlpools that take heavy toll of life and merchandise from those who enter, thus creating the tradition that only the hardy and the favored of the gods pass through.

Such is the entrance to the country which the first Western traveler, Marco Polo, who visited that country in the thirteenth century, described as a cultivated garden with great cities, and a recent visitor calls "Sze-chuan the Beautiful, the richest and most populous and altogether the most picturesque part of China."

For many centuries and until yesterday, the journey from Ichang to Chung-king, a distance of 500 miles, required fully a month and sometimes two. It was made by native junk, pulled along after the manner of the old-fashioned canal-boat, but, instead of the tow-path mule, by a crew of twenty to sixty men tugging at the shore end of a bamboo hawser sometimes fully one-half mile in length.

The task of these trackers is most arduous and beset with constant danger. Sometimes they are seen scrambling over rocks and boulders upon which it would seem impossible for men to travel; next we see them clinging to the sides of precipitous cliffs where a slip costs a limb or a life; and again set on all fours, gripping fast to rock or shore, while the crew aboard the boat pries it obliquely into and up the stream by the bow-sweep set against the onrushing current; then plunging forward under the lash of the fu-teo to gain headway as the boat is released and swings shoreward.

RIVER BOATS AT ICHANG, ON THE YANGTZE, AT THE FOOT OF THE GORGES

Note the newly bought, heavy coils of woven bamboo cable which are used for towing the boat over the rapids. From twenty to fifty men are required for each boat at many of the rapids. According to an official guide-book, the Yangtze has almost as many names "as a cat has lives." Over the greater portion of its more than 3000-mile course it is known to the Chinese as Kiang or Chiang (River *par excellence*), the Ta-kiang (Large River) or the Chang-kiang (Long River). In Tibet it is the Murus, in Sze-chuan and Yunnan it is the Chin-sha-kialig (Gold Sand River), and after entering the province of Kiangsu it is the Yangtze-kiang (Child of the Ocean).

Today, dynamite is blasting a safer course, and fourteen-knot steamers make the journey in forty steaming hours. The devils of the waters, as these rivermen will believe, have won their victories also, for a large German commercial steamer lies buried in 120 feet of water at the entrance to one of the gorges.

Tomorrow it will be the railway, for it is now known that Sze-chuan holds a golden store for the first road that enters it. The French have long planned to extend their Tongking-Yunnan line northwest to Chung-king and Cheng-tu.

The Belgian syndicate has contracted for a line southwest from Singan to Cheng-tu, which will connect the province with the railway systems of northeast China and Manchuria; and the Four-nation Hu-Kwang agreement, in which America has a share, calls for a line from Han-kow to Cheng-tu.

A company of American engineers has completed the survey of this last named line and a start has been made on its construction. When this is completed it will be supper in Ichang, breakfast in Chung-king, and tiffin in Cheng-tu.

A FISHING BOAT IN THE YANGTZE GORGES AND A JUNK WITH THE SMALL
SAIL OF MATTING WHICH IS OFTEN USED TO SUPPLEMENT COOLIE POWER

Note the ponderous fish-net, a type in use throughout China. The frame works on a hinge. The net is lowered
into the water, and when the fisherman thinks the sought-for fish are above it, he raises it by means of a lever
arm and scoops out his "catch."

THE SPIRIT OF THE ORIENT DEPARTS WHEN THE LOCOMOTIVE ENTERS

Time, which in the West is born with wings and flies, but in China stands footless, content to crawl, will be saved, and the Szechuan Alps will vie with those of Europe as the Mecca of travelers. But with the gain will come the loss of the most extraordinary journey in the world, for the spirit of the Orient departs when the locomotive enters.

Gone will be that growing sense of the grandeur and majesty of God's creation, which is experienced as one moves slowly through these gorges to their climax in the Woosang Gorge, where thirteen peaks rise one above another five thousand feet into the clouds.

No longer will there be the thrill of danger overcome, and one will not hear the weird antiphonal songs of the boatmen as they ply the oar or swing along the shore, nor join in their whistled prayer as they call to the spirit-winds for a favor in the gorges.

We shall miss the bang-bang of the firecrackers, set off from the rear of the boat to loose the grip of the demons that hold us fast in

"FISH-TAIL" BOATS ON THE YANGTZE AT THE ENTRANCE
TO THE UPPERMOST OF THE FAMOUS "THREE GORGES"

For centuries the main artery of commerce for the great province of Sze-chuan, with a population equal to half that of the United States, has been through the gorges of the Yangtze, where the coolie matches his strength against that of the rapids, as he and his kind tow heavily laden vessels from Ichang to Chung-king, a distance of 500 miles, in which the river has a fall of 500 feet.

TRACKERS ON THE YANGTZE TAKING THEIR NOONDAY MEAL

The river boats are hauled through the gorges of the Yangtze by these trackers, who tug at the shore end of a bamboo hawser sometimes half a mile in length.

A DIFFICULT STRETCH OF TOW-PATH ALONG THE YANGTZE

"Gripping fast to the rocks, where a slip costs a limb or a life."

THE WEST CHINA JITNEY

THE "BACK OF MAN" IS THE UNWRITTEN EPIC OF SZE-CHUAN

Coal and other minerals from the mountains, wood from the hills, the merchandise of cities, the grain of the plain, even the pigs en route to market and the men who can afford the fee—all ride on the back of man.

AS THERE IS NO WHEELED TRAFFIC IN SZE-CHUAN EXCEPT BY WHEELBARROW,
THE HIGHWAYS OVER THE HILLS OFTEN CONSIST OF A SERIES OF STEPS.

the rapids, and we shall miss the odor of the incense burned at the bow as a favor to the gods.

Such passing sights as the trained cormorant catching fish for his master, the gold-washers scouring the gravel for its gold, and the daily sport of half a hundred men struggling to be the first to devour his morning rice will not be encountered or enjoyed. Neither can we challenge another boat, bearing another flag, for a thirty days' race to the city of Chung-king, and reap the joy of finishing with the Stars and Stripes waving a salute to a worthy foeman less than one hundred feet behind at the end of the five-hundred-mile journey.

CHUNG-KING AND BEYOND

Chung-king, at which we have arrived, is a walled city with 600,000 inhabitants, situated at the confluence of the Yangtze and the Kia-ling rivers, and is, through the fiction of a foreign treaty, an open seaport, notwithstanding the fact that it is 1,500 miles from the coast and 1,000 feet above the level of the sea. It is now the head of steam navigation for nearly a dozen steamers controlled by the Chinese, the seat of maritime customs for the West, the point of distribution for all western-borne commerce and the assembling depot for all shipments to other parts of China and foreign lands.

A PART OF CHUNG-KING'S CITY OF THE DEAD

Every mound and white spot in sight marks a grave. Around Chung-king there are miles and miles of these graves—and no one knows how many layers deep!

The chief exports to America and other countries are paint oils of the tung-tree, medicines, bristles, feathers, and hides, and, of manufactured articles, silks, satins, and crêpes of the finest grades.

Confined between its two rivers, this city, like New York, is growing into the air. It has no suburban lines to relieve its surplus population, and real estate has accordingly increased in the past decade from 100 to 200 per cent in value, making it profitable to erect fine foreign buildings, in which it excels any purely native city in China.

The English, French, German, Japanese, and Americans have had gunboats anchored on its rivers and are competing for its trade, with the English in the lead. United States trade is represented in kerosene, sewing-machines, cigarettes, patent medicines, hardware, and nails.

A 300-MILE TRIP IN A SEDAN-CHAIR

From Chung-king northwestward 300 miles to Cheng-tu we travel by sedan-chair, borne on the shoulders of two, three, or four bearers, as one's avoirdupois requires or his

THE FOOT THAT PLIES THE PUMP CONTROLS THE CROP IN MANY PARTS OF CHINA

These particular coolies do not seem to be downcast by the monotony or the strenuousness of their share in the task of irrigation, however.

PLOWING UNDER WATER AND UNDER DIFFICULTIES IN THE CHENG-TU PLAIN

The farmer of the Cheng-tu Plain knows little of the science of gardening, but much of its method. He has made Sze-chuan, known as the Garden of Asia, where famine never comes.

HAYSTACKS TIED TO TREES IN THE PADDY FIELD OF A SZE-CHUAN FARM

As the farmer needs hay he takes it from the bottom of the stack, permitting the weathered portion to remain. The embankment paths separating the paddy fields are bordered with bean plants.

Troy weight permits; for the rich ride in fours by choice, as do the portly without option.

In addition to the chair-bearers, the foreign traveler requires a coolie to bear his cot and bedding, another to carry his food, and an attendant to cook it. A small party easily becomes a regiment, and if an armed escort accompanies it, as is usual, the party resembles an army.

Beyond the walls of Chung-king we enter the city of the dead. We pass square-built tombs of the Ming period; near by are the crowded lines of public graves for, beggars and the very poor; and then, far away to the top of the hill, about four miles distant, are the regulation mounds of Chinese graves, with here and there beautifully carved, terraced mausoleums.

A more orderly section of broad extent, reserved for Mohammedan graves, shows that the followers of the Crescent are no mean or inconsiderable company among the city's population.

Over these sleeping camps the telegraph lines are now strung and the Cheng-tu Railway will tunnel beneath them. Factories and homes are pushing them farther from the city, which is a sure indication that the hand of superstition is losing its grip, for a quarter century ago this would have spelled r-i-o-t.

THE CONVOLUTIONS OF SZE-CHUAN
PADDY FIELDS ARE WONDERFUL IN SYMMETRY

Much of the tillable area of this province of China is extremely hilly. The rice fields must be terraced and the water lifted to them by man-power.

The Sze-chuanese of old have been expert workers in stone, as is evidenced by the many tombs, homes, and places of defense carved deep into the rocky cliffs along the rivers. Their Chinese conquerors have inherited this art along with their land, for the country abounds with artistically carved stone bridges and memorial arches of massive proportions ornately wrought in stone.

One never sees a monument dedicated to a warrior, but many to virtuous widows, who refused to remarry after their husbands had died. Others reared by royal permit have the four characters *Wu Kia Tung Tang*, five genera-tions living together in one home. This, though not common, is by no means unknown in West China, and surely, if five generations can live together in one home and live peaceably, they deserve recognition, and the Chinese accord it, as these massive stone and tile mosaic monu-ments attest.

THE LAND OF PAGODAS

West China might be called "The Land of the Pagoda," for nearly every city has its tower-ing sentinel from three to fifteen stories in height. They are generally placed upon some eminence overlooking the city they protect, and may have served as watch-towers in times of trouble, but the real purpose of their erection most likely was to exert a benign influence upon the fung suei—the spirits of wind and wave that bring prosperity and ward off disaster.

Out from the crush and the hum of the city of the living and past the quiet camp of the dead, we come to the country—not, however, the country of the Western world; rather a mass of terraced paddy fields and farm gardens, with human beings always in sight. People are the only feature of the landscape that we cannot leave behind or ignore, so we stop here in our journey to glance at the inhabitants of Sze-chuan, who surpass in rugged diversity of race the variety of the province's scenery.

More valuable than its rich mineral deposits and superbly tilled land, the people of Sze-chuan are at once its prime asset and interest.

THE FOUR EPOCHS
OF THE SZE-CHUANESE

Four epochs mark the Sze-chuanese and help to explain them:

First, the slow retreat of the ancient aborigines up into the mountains of the south and west and the occupation of the fertile land by the oncoming victorious Chinese.

Second, the ruthless Chinese wars, culminating in the ravages of the tyrant Chang, who, in accordance with his slogan, "Kill! Kill! Kill! Kill! Kill! Kill! Kill! for all men are evil," left many of its cities desolate and its fields without inhabitants.

Third, the repeopling of the province by emigrants from the north, central, and south-eastern provinces of China, who, fusing with the scattered Chinese and aboriginal inhabitants and with Mohammedan mercenaries from western Asia, formed the composite Sze-chuanese, styled "Chinese, with a difference."

Fourth, the contact of Christian life and thought upon these peoples, a period of reforms and revolutions, a transition from the old order to the New China of today and the China of promise of tomorrow.

Prof. Edward A. Ross, author of "The Changing Chinese," says of them:

"Those who have known these people longest question whether in a match on even terms our own race could keep up with them. Their physiognomy tends to be intellectual and refined, with little of the Mongolian cast of feature. One comes on youthful shepherds who recall the wonderful shepherd Antinous, who became the favorite of the Emperor Hadrian.

"Oval faces with penciled, arching eyebrows, fine eyes, delicate temples, straight noses with high-cut nostrils, challenge one's notion that male beauty went out with the Greeks.

"THE MUSEUM OF
THE HUMAN RACES"

It is this complex human amalgam that we call the Sze-chuanese who occupy the eastern half of the province.

The western part of Sze-chuan might well be called the Museum of the Human Races, the as-yet-undiscovered happy hunting-ground of the ethnologist and physiognomist. Here are to be found the surviving remnants in the most heroic struggle for existence that humanity has ever waged and who, for lack of a better term, we call the "Tribesmen."

As we cross the Min River, which, flowing south, divides the province into east and west,

WEIGHING SALT AS IT COMES IN CAKES FROM EVAPORATION VATS: CHINA

Tszlinching, in the province of Sze-chuan, is one of the chief centers of the salt industry in China. Here a forest of derricks suggests one of our own oil-boom towns. The wells have been drilled by foot-power to a depth of from 2,400 to 2,800 feet (see text, page 38).

and move westward, toward the snow-covered mountains, we come upon the shambling homes of these people, hidden in impassable ravines or perched upon cliff or mountain side, of which they seem to be part and counterpart; for as the irresistible side-thrust of continental Asia pushed these mountain masses high into the snows and left them crumpled, broken, and isolated stormswept peaks, so, evidently a similar convulsion of powerful peoples of Asia, in their movements toward this center, have driven back the weaker or defenseless nations, they in their turn being compelled to follow into these inaccessible places, where, like the mountains to which they still cling, they may yet reveal for us, stratum by stratum, the bedrock of the race.

"THE SZE-CHUAN TRIBESMEN"

The Chinese call them "The Eighteen Nations," but it is believed that there are several times eighteen nations or tribes, each under its own king, council, or feudal lord, independent or semi-independent of each other and of the Chinese in whose borders they dwell.

Among the tribesmen are found representatives of the black, yellow, and white branches of the human family, and some of them, especially the dwarf peoples, are believed to be of very ancient origin.

On the western side these Sze-chuanese are flanked by the Tibetans, who have spread their religious ideas among many of them. Litang, the best known of the border lamaseries, is situated in one of the mountain passes on the roof of the world at an elevation of 14,000 feet. Here, in this sparsely settled country, there are crowded together not less than three thousand lamas.

Returning to the big road to Cheng-tu, we stop to notice the swiftly moving army of carriers, each with his minimum load of 106 pounds on an average journey of thirty miles.

Nothing is on wheels. Not a wheeled vehicle is seen in all West China except the wheelbarrow, near Cheng-tu. Thousands of tons of commerce pass over these highways annually, all on the backs of men; and as we approach the centers of population we find the sewage and the water of the city are on their backs also.

A NATION ON THE BACKS OF MEN

The "Back of Man" is the unwritten epic of this land; for, Atlas-like, it bears the world upon it. The coal and other minerals from the mountains; the cities, with their walls and towers and all that they contain; the wood on the hills and the grain of the plain—all, together with the pigs en route to market and the men who can afford it—all have ridden or ride upon the back of man.

The reason is not far to seek. It is purely economic. Man is the most efficient machine and the cheapest animal, and so it comes to pass that he is the universal animal, the omnibus of commerce and the pack-mule of the race.

It is cheaper to wear men down than keep roads up. When he falls, few care and still fewer pity, for others are eager to fill his place. Should we offer to take the burden from his shoulder, he would regard it as taking the rice from his bowl.

Sharing with these carriers the burden of the nation's life is the proverbial "Man with the Hoe," usually a poor tenant giving half his crop for the rent of his acre. Frequently, however, he is able to own his own implements and a water-buffalo, with which he plows his own and his neighbor's plot, receiving in turn his neighbor's help in seed-time and harvest.

Still others, and on the rich Cheng-tu plain they are numerous, are wealthy farmers, who live in fine homes and till their estates with the help of sons and grandsons or with hired servants.

To these farmers is given the task of feeding a nation of 60,000,000 people; for Sze-chuan, isolated by mountain barriers, must be self-sustaining. The measure of this task is appreciated when we consider that fully 50 per cent of the 181,000 square miles of Sze-chuan is too mountainous for cultivation, which means that these sixty millions are sustained on an area less than one-half that of the State of Texas.

Add to this condition his lack of scientific knowledge and the primitive implements with which he labors, as well as the necessity of

AN ALL-BAMBOO IRRIGATION WATER-WHEEL IN THE CHENG-TU PLAIN, SIMILAR
TO THE ENORMOUS WATER-WHEELS ON THE ORONTES RIVER AT HAMAH, SYRIA
The Cheng-tu Plain is said to have one of the most ancient systems of irrigation in the world. It was perfected
about 200 B. C. by Li Ping, now recognized as the patron saint of the capital of Sze-chuan and Tibet.

securing and returning to the soil, as fertilizers, all that he reaps from it; remember, also, that rice, his chief cereal crop, is the most difficult of all cereals to produce, especially in a country where the hills must be terraced and water lifted to fill the paddy fields, and it becomes evident that the Sze-chuan farmer's task is next to impossible and its accomplishment little short of a miracle.

He is, however, favored with a temperate climate all the year and a naturally rich soil, an atmosphere saturated with moisture, an abundant rainfall, and a never-failing supply of water for irrigation from the melting snows on the mountains near by.

He produces nearly every vegetable and grain found in our market and others to which we are strangers. The fruits that are ours are his also. Apples are few and poor in quality, but the persimmon and orange are second to none and are produced in great abundance. One thousand oranges on the upper Yangtze can be purchased for 50 cents.

He knows little of the science of gardening, but much of its method. By interplanting, especially beans and peas, which he knows improves the quality of the soil, by crop rotation, which he knows increases his yield, and by intensive fertilizing and the sowing of vetch in the fallow season, he manages to keep his fields rich and raises from two to six crops a year. He has made Sze-chuan known as the Garden of Asia, the land where famine never comes.

RICE: THE MASTER CROP

The tenant farmer pays his rent with the major portion of his rice, which is the master crop and his chief concern and joy in life. In the early spring he plows his paddy fields, and then prays for rains to flood them, offering incense to the god of the garden, whose shrine is built near by.

When rain and gods fail him, he sets to work with endless-chain, foot-treadle pumps, laboriously lifting into his terraced fields the water that he has conserved in the valley. Then, breaking up the rice sod, which has been grown from early sowing in highly fertilized plots, he transplants it in hills in the watered paddy fields.

The roily water makes the hoeing of his rice field impossible; so he does not hoe it; he toes it. With bare foot he feels about the plant with his toes, and if he finds a weed, he toes it out; then presses the dirt firmly in place again. With his right foot he toes two rows, with his left foot he toes two rows, and thus he toes four rows as he goes. That's the way he hoes.

Then come the tares, which the novice cannot distinguish from the rice. Unlike the Bible story, he does not leave them till the harvest, but pulls them loose and casts them upon the highway to be trodden under foot.

For the harvest the farmers combine and render mutual assistance. The rice is cut with the sickle, gathered in bundles, and the grain beaten out by striking it upon slats in the center of a large bin which is pulled along after the threshers.

Dried upon bamboo mats, rolled and cleaned, it is then ready to be transported to market.

The native's fondness for rice is proverbial. Corn and wheat he regards as poor substitutes, and sweet potatoes too plebeian for any but the beggar to enjoy.

THE WONDERFUL
SALT WELLS OF SZE-CHUAN

About midway between Chung-king and Cheng-tu we are tempted by the long trains of salt carriers to turn aside and see the renowned salt industry at Tszliuching, which means "Flowing Well." Its origin is lost in antiquity, being first mentioned in the reign of the Minor Han Dynasty in Sze-chuan, A. D. 221-263.

With its forest of derricks it resembles an oil boom town. The wells have been drilled by foot-power to a depth of 2,400 feet for brine and about 2,800 for natural gas, which is used exclusively for the evaporation of the brine.

Salt is the unfailing source of government revenue and its production is guarded most jealously to prevent monopoly.

The proprietor of the salt well cannot own a gas well or evaporating plant. Likewise, the owner of the gas well or evaporating pans cannot engage in the other branches of the industry, thus making each dependent upon the other and preventing family or government control.

There are no flowing wells now, the brine being lifted in bamboo buckets about 50 feet in length and four to five inches in diameter. The power is supplied by water-buffaloes, hitched in fours to a 60-foot horizontal drum, about which the rope fastened to the bucket winds as the animals are beaten around the circle at a wild gallop. The magnitude of the industry may be gleaned from the fact that every family demands its weekly pound of salt, and that many tons are exported each month to other provinces.

A CABLE BRIDGE OF BAMBOO IN NORTHERN SZE-CHUAN
The top cables are eight inches in diameter. On the bottom cables are laid transverse boards.

THE "EMBROIDERED CITY" IN A FERTILE PLAIN

Returning once more to the Big Road and passing without comment its towns and cities, located about ten miles apart, we come to Cheng-tu, the Perfect Capital, a vice-regal city of half a million people, ruling over Sze-chuan and Tibet. It is surrounded by a finely constructed brick wall, 35 to 40 feet in height, with a thickness at the top of 20 feet and a circumference of more than nine miles.

Cheng-tu is an ancient capital, its first recorded wall being built 2,315 years ago. Marco Polo described it as a trinity of cities beautifully embellished. Its approaches were carved marble bridges which spanned its moat.

Its wall, nearly 20 miles in circumference, inclosing a population of more than a million, was surrounded by rows of hibiscus trees which in autumn bloom made it the "Embroidered City," a name that has long outlived the wall and its trees. Some conception of the toil required to erect such a wall may be gained from the historical records, which state that the construction of one of its extensions, eight miles in length, required an army of 100,000 men and 9,600,000 days' work.

Cheng-tu has given its name to the plain on which it stands.

This plain is said to have one of the finest and most ancient systems of irrigation in the world. It was perfected about 200 B. C. by Li Ping, who has since become the patron saint of

A LUSTY-LUNGED SON OF SZE-CHUAN

Cheng-tu—the only instance of which I am aware where a civil engineer has become a patron saint. He divided the Min into three great delta systems of rivers and canals, which radiate to all parts of the 80-mile plain. The waters are united again in two main streams, which leave the southwest and southeast borders of the plain by the Min and the Lin rivers. He left the people this motto for regulating the canals: "Keep the banks low and the bottom clean;" and this wise counsel has prevented the disastrous floods of ancient times, while furnishing a never-failing supply of mountain water for the fields.

AMERICAN EDUCATIONAL INFLUENCES

It is not, however, this fertile plain, with its irrigation and teeming millions; nor the city, with its ancient culture and modern shops; nor yet this wall, upon whose battlements we lean,

A MEDICINE MAN OF THE CHENG-TU PLAIN

that claims chief consideration, but a modern institution rising just beside it; for, interesting as is Old China, with its walled-in peoples and civilization, it holds, no such world significance as the China of today, which such institutions have in large measure made possible.

We are familiar with the magnitude and importance of the work of American colleges at Constantinople and Beirut, in the Near East; but the far-reaching and beneficent work of the Christian colleges in the Far East is not so gen-erally recognized. In marked contrast to the European missionaries, who have placed com-paratively little emphasis on education in China, and especially higher education, the American missionary enterprise and Christian education have from the first been inseparable and almost synonymous.

In the training of China's sons the Ameri-can missionary not only prepared many of the men who have taken high place in the life of the nation, but he created the impulse that led

"West to the sinking sun,
Where the junk sails lift
Through the homeless drift
And the East and the West are one."

LITTLE CELESTIALS AT PLAY

Chinese little folks are protected from the cold not by woolen garments, but by an increased number of layers of clothing, which gives them a humorous appearance of roundness.

the sons of its first families to America to complete their education.

When the Manchu Dynasty was overthrown and China was floundering headlessly about, seeking to establish a new dynasty or to re-establish the old Han Dynasty of 4,600 years ago, it was a small group of men trained in Christian and American colleges who were the Jefferson and Hamilton of the Chinese Constitution and who brought the most ancient of monarchical countries in line with the democracy of our day.

The intimate relation of the Christian college to the progress of the nation is not, however, limited to parliament. Graduates of these colleges are superintending its great iron and steel plants, directing its railways and telegraphs; holding portfolios in the cabinet and sitting upon the Supreme Bench; directing

THE WATER GATE SPRING

Fantasy of form and variety of hue lurk in every nook and corner of China's cities. Merrily upturned pagoda roofs and gay lanterns vie with bright costumes. Her centuries of accumulated beauty will give the world joy through a long forever.

in large measure the educational policy of the nation and bearing their full share of the spiritual responsibilities in the church, the Christian schools, and the Y. M. C. A. Should we look into the embassiesn, we meet Dr. V. K. Wellington Koo at Washington and at London Hon. Alfred S. K. Sze, M. A., both graduates of a Chinese Christian college.

CHANGING CUSTOMS IN CHINA

Ignorance, which breeds superstition and bolsters wrong, is not confined to China, but it has found Christian education in that nation its worst enemy. Many of the gods of yesterday have been tumbled into the ash-heap to make way for the school-boy with his books, and

COOLIES WITH BAMBOO PRODUCTS: MIN VALLEY, SZE-CHUAN

Bamboo is used endlessly in China, and here are sandals, hats, sheaths, carrying poles and even a pipe made of this ubiquitous plant. Its fruit, tender shoots and seeds are used for food, and the Chinese have a belief that it produces grain more plentifully in the years when the rice crop fails.

what was religion to many yesterday is useless superstition today.

Customs that were respected hitherto are now despised. For centuries little children have been bound at the altar of custom to hobble with constricted feet to a painful old age. Preaching and protest went unheeded until the Christian girls' schools demonstrated that big-footed women were the queens of the land, not its slaves. Students now in government schools are announcing that they will not marry girls who have not natural feet, and girls with bound feet parade the streets with their little feet in big boots.

The reason is evident. Big feet and brains have come to be synonymous. Government schools are refusing admission to bound-footed girls, and the better classes are in the big-foot crusade. Women in useful service have come with the new order.

THE DRAGON RAPIDS OF THE YANGTZE

The great river takes its upper course through a succession of magnificent gorges, past cities set picturesquely among the mountains and an occasional temple capping a crag. Harnessed to a bamboo cable, the trackers in the picture are hauling a junk through the perilous rapids.

BOAT DWELLERS AT CANTON

The Tan-min or inmates of the river boats are a strange class, long regarded as outcast, who live by the carrying trade. From birth to death, their crowded, turbulent lives are spent upon the river. Tradition says they originated from political refugees.

AN O-MA-TO-FU STONE

The stone marks the resort of a kindly spirit. With its terrific carven features incongruously sheltered by straw hats, the image inspires an Occidental with irreverent amusement, which at least one little Chinaman seems to share. The red-tipped prayer sticks have been placed here, however, by one more devout.

THE BRIDGE AT WAN-HSIEN, SZE-CHUAN

Not even the handiwork of Nature in rushing water and towering rock is more beautiful than the stone arches that span the many streams of Sze-chuan province the—"western East." The bridge at Wan-hsien is one of the most graceful.

A COOLIE AND HIS BURDEN

Among the burden-bearers of mountainous Sze-chuan are to be found examples of magnificent power and physique.

WIDOWS' MONUMENTS IN YEN-CHAU

No medieval craftsman decorating a beloved cathedral ever wrought with more devotion to every detail, more delicacy and finish, even in hidden and shadowy parts, than do the builders of these beautiful arches.

YOUNG CHINA

Here is a type of Chinese childhood as light-hearted and active as any European or American boy. Too often the struggle against want crushes out youthful qualities at an early age, giving rise to the generalization that Chinese children are not inclined to sport and exercise.

THE TSIEN-TANG RIVER NEAR HANG-CHAU

Legend says that the tidal bore for which Hang-chau is famous is really the spectre of the Prince Tse Hsu riding up the river. The mighty wave crest seen by the light of the moon has a ghostly majesty and fury suggestive of the warrior prince.

A STREET IN PEKING

Past and present, the picturesque and the everyday are mingled in the Chinese capital. Here is an improved and very modern highway, and a springless Peking cart which would insure a rough ride on the smoothest road.

A COVERED BRIDGE WEST OF CHUNG-KING

The more fortunate residents of Chung-king, during the warm, moist summer, escape from the crowded city to the surrounding, delightful hill country. Through a vista at the left may be seen sedan chairs and their bearers on the road.

THE GREAT SIX HARMONY PAGODA NEAR HANG-CHAU

The stately pagoda is supposed to control the winds and the turbulent waters of the Tsien-tang. While many may doubt its mystic influence, none can deny the loveliness of the scene it commands from the tree-clad bank of the broad river.

OUTSIDE THE WALLS OF CHUNG-KING

Chung-king is China's Pittsburgh, a great, busy, crowded, foggy city at the junction of the Yangtze and the Kia-ling. Its grim wall, steep, rocky streets, great flights of wet stone, steps up which the water supply is carried by man power, and the turmoil and complexity of its commerce are the antithesis of the Pennsylvanian mart, but characteristic of interior China.

THE WORLD'S ANCIENT PORCELAIN CENTER

BY FRANK B. LENZ
With Illustrations from Photographs by the Author

CHINA is a land of literature, art, and scholarship. It is also a land of ignorance, superstition, and misery. It is the country made famous by the printing-press, mariner's compass, gunpowder, the Great Wall, tea, silk, jade, paper, and ancient porcelain; it is the home of plague, famine, intrigue, flood, graft, and corruption.

Conservative of the conservatives, it is also a radical among radicals. One sees in every city ancient, decaying temples, with their oriental systems of religion gradually giving way to the progressive, onward march of civilization. Change, change; nothing is permanent in China but change.

Industrially the country is in the same state that Europe was in before the approach of the industrial revolution. It is in the handicraft stage of development; but in cities like Canton, Shanghai, Hankow, Changsha, and Tientsin the most modern machinery of the twentieth century is seen in operation every day. This is not China. The real China has yet to learn the value of the machine.

FOUR-FIFTHS OF CHINA'S POPULATION IS DEVOTED TO MANUAL LABOR

Perhaps the only factor which permits China to compete in a commercial way with the rest of the world is its cheapness of labor.

It has been repeatedly said that the cheapest and most abundant thing in the country is human life. The common man of the farm or of the city is the coolie, properly called "k'u li," or, better, strength. When we reflect that 80 per cent of China's vast population is forced to labor hard, barehanded, for a mere physical existence, we can begin to grasp the significance of its industrial situation. No modern inventions; no machines have come to set it free. Like Edwin Markham's "Man with the Hoe," the Chinese worker feels the weight of centuries of toil upon his shoulders.

The economic problem today is tragic, and were it not for its natural characteristic of patience, China would be in the throes of a bloody revolution.

ARTISTS ENGAGED IN DECORATING PORCELAIN
IN ONE OF CHING-TEH-CHEN'S LARGEST FACTORIES

Note the thousands of pieces stored overhead, all awaiting the under-glaze decoration. After being decorated, the glaze is applied in one of several ways—by dipping, by being blown on through a tube, or by sprinkling. The piece is then ready for the furnace.

A BIRD'S-EYE VIEW OF CHING-TEH-CHEN SHOWING SOME OF ITS CHIMNEYS

THE HOME OF THE WORLD'S PORCELAIN INDUSTRY

The greatest industrial city of China is not one of the treaty ports, where the direct influence of Western progress is constantly felt, but a bustling interior city of Kiangsi Province—Ching-teh-chen.* This is the famous porcelain and pottery center of the nation—indeed, it is the original home of the porcelain industry of the world.

There are few cities in America or Europe that are so completely given over to a single industry as this one. Though the methods of production are primitive, the city must still be classed as an industrial center. It was my rare privilege to visit this conservative, but interest-ing, old place and see with my own eyes the fascinating process of pottery-making from beginning to end.

Chinaware! What does the word connote? It is simply a ware made of clay and named for the country that first produced it. Whether it be a green tile from a temple roof, a dish, a vase, or a painted ornament from a wealthy Celestial's home, it all has a traceable connection with Ching-teh-chen. With the Chinese, Ching-teh-chen and porcelain are synonymous.

In order to get a fair understanding of the situation, it will first be necessary to let the reader know the location of this place and something of the difficulties in reaching it.

HOW TO REACH, CHING-TEH-CHEN

After locating Shanghai on the map of China, one should trace his way up the Yangtze

*The city is designated on many maps as King-teh-chen, King-te-chen, or Chang-nan-chen.

BOATS LOADED WITH SOFT, WHITE CLAY BRICKS FOR THE PORCELAIN FACTORIES
The mounds in the background are not gravel, but piles of porcelain debris, broken cups, etc.

River to Kiukiang, south of which lies Po Yang Lake. The quickest and surest way of reaching Ching-teh-chen is to proceed from Kiukiang to Nanchang, the capital of the province, by rail. This trip can be made in a day, barring accidents, though the distance is only 90 miles. In no respect an industrial center, Nanchang has many wonderful porcelain shops, all supplied by the factories of the porcelain city.

In prospect it did not seem a difficult task to cover the distance between Nanchang and Ching- teh-chen, 120 miles, but in reality the trip required more time than it takes to travel from San Francisco to New York. One must cross the east end of Po Yang Lake and then push his way up the North River into the heart of the mountains, to a point not far from the Anhwei border.

Traveling by a small and rickety steam-launch, which was completely covered with a cargo of human freight, we left Nanchang, passed down the Kan River and out across the lake. It was 8 o'clock on a June morning and the thermometer registered 90 degrees.

We steamed merrily along until noon, when we suddenly struck a mud flat. My heart sank as numerous stories of people stranded for several days in the middle of this vast stretch of shallow water flashed into my mind.

THOUSANDS OF BOATS ARE ENGAGED IN
HAULING WOOD FOR THE PORCELAIN FURNACES

Only straw and wood can be used in firing chinaware. Coal has been tried, but its fumes discolored the porcelain.

Fortunately, we were running at half speed, and after violently churning up the mud we were able to back off and strike a new course, sounding our way until we entered the mouth of the river leading to Raochow, the most important city on the lake.

TRAVEL ON A CHINESE HOUSE-BOAT

At Raochow (also spelled Juichow and Jaochou) our house-boat experience began. With the assistance of the water police captain, we at once transferred to a small but comfortable boat. It was not, however, until after nearly an hour's delay, due to the necessity of purchasing some eggs, vegetables, and charcoal for the journey, that we started upstream against a swiftly running current, just as the stars came out.

The police captain had been informed by wire of our coming and was waiting for us with a guard. These guards are stationed at intervals along the river in "p'ao Ch'uan," or gunboats, and are supposed to help in the collection of the revenue tax and to protect travelers from bandits.

The single unarmed soldier who was provided for our protection proved very useful in steering the boat while the three boatmen

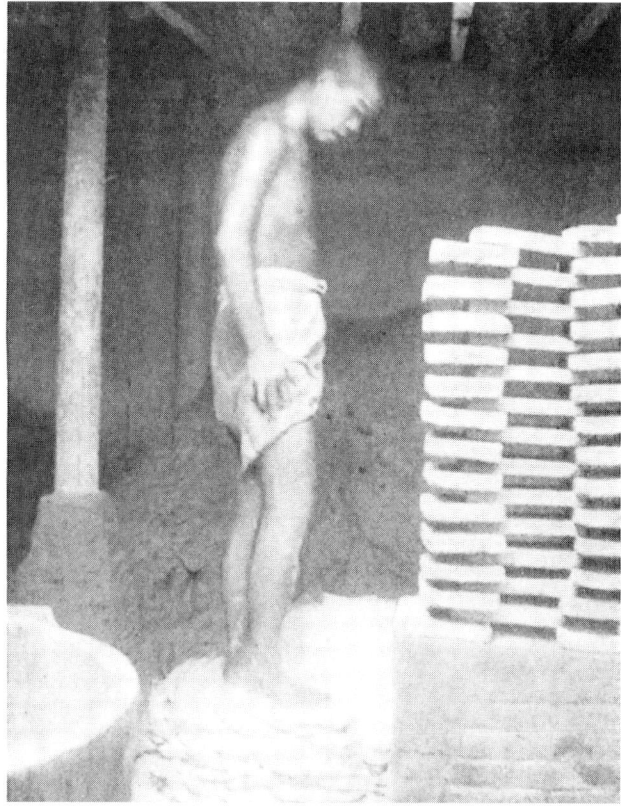

KNEADING CLAY BY FOOT-POWER AFTER IT
HAS BEEN THOROUGHLY CLEANSED AND SIFTED

After the soft clay bricks have been brought from the quarries, they are "worked up" in this manner until the material is ready for the potter's wheel. More than a dozen kinds of clay are found in the neighborhood of Po Yang Lake.

paddled, poled, and pulled our craft up into the higher reaches of the stream.

All night long they worked, now and then singing, first to the water spirits and then to the spirits in the heavens. After an interval of rowing for a mile or more, the boatmen would rest by getting out and taking the boat in tow with a long rope attached to the mast, while the guard sat in the stern at the rudder and kept us away from the shore.

The craft itself was about 40 feet long and was divided into three sections, with space in each for two "p'u kais," or mattresses. In the stern, covered with boards, was a charcoal stove, with an ample supply of rice near by. The principal articles of food were eggs, rice, fish, several kinds of vegetables, and tea—good, substantial food when one is living in the open. By removing the floor and standing on the bottom of the boat, one could assume an erect position with ease.

THIS MILK-LIKE LIQUID IS THE PORCELAIN GLAZE READY
TO BE BLOWN OR BRUSHED UPON THF POTTERS' PRODUCT

The Chinese porcelain makers pursue their occupation today with practically the same implements which they have employed for 1,700 years. There are probably fewer mechanical devices in use in Ching-teh-chen than in any other industrial city of its size in the world.

Life on a house-boat means an abundance of fresh air and freedom from the ever-present and noisy Chinese crowd. To appreciate its comforts, one must make the boat his dwelling-place long enough to grow attached to it.

Late in the afternoon of the second day out from Raochow we approached Ching-teh-chen. I shall never forget the thrill I experienced as I first caught sight of the smoke issuing from the chimneys of scores of kilns.

Quite an ordinary scene in any Western industrial city, but here, far away from the main routes of travel, in a conservative, interior province of China, it was as striking as it was unusual.

The first view one gets of any Chinese city is likely to be the bold outline of a tower or temple, but in Ching-teh-chen the first thing that caught our expectant gaze was something entirely different.

MIXING PORCELAIN CLAYS: CHING-TEH-CHEN

Some clays are brittle, some are tough. This is the method of mixing used in all the factories (see text, page 68).

A CITY WONDERFULLY SITUATED

The situation of Ching-teh-chen is perfect, from the Chinese point of view. The city is located between the mouths of two rivers which flow into the North River, one from the east and one from the west. The town is naturally supplied with an abundance of fresh water, the clearness of which still stands out in my mind in vivid contrast to the muddy yellowness of the Yangtze and of Po Yang Lake.

Beautiful hills completely surrounded the city, those on the east rising to a height of about two thousand feet. The river banks are dotted with pine and camphor trees, while occasional groves of bamboo in lighter green add a charm and beauty difficult to describe. For most of my life I have lived among the giant redwoods of northern California, the stateliness and vastness of which have always deeply moved me. In them I saw strength and power. But in the groves and trees of Kiangsi I found a softness and beauty typical of another world—a tropical world.

LONGFELLOW PAID TRIBUTE TO CHING-TEH-CHEN

Ching-teh-chen ("Town of Scenic Virtue,") is one of the four largest towns of China. Technically, it is a town, because it has no wall. In reality it is a busy industrial city of 300,000

THE POTTER AT HIS WHEEL

After placing the ball of soft clay on the knob of the rapidly revolving wheel, he deftly forms a cup, vase, or bowl with mechanical precision.

people, two-thirds of whom are engaged in the manufacture and sale of porcelain. Romantically, it is a city to stir men's souls. Longfellow, in his "Keramos," speaks of it in these words:

"And bird-like, poise on balanced wing
Above the town of King-te-tching,
A burning town, or seeming so,—
Three thousand furnaces that glow
Incessantly, and fill the air
With smoke uprising, gyre on gyre,
And painted by the lurid glare,
Of jets and flashes of red fire."

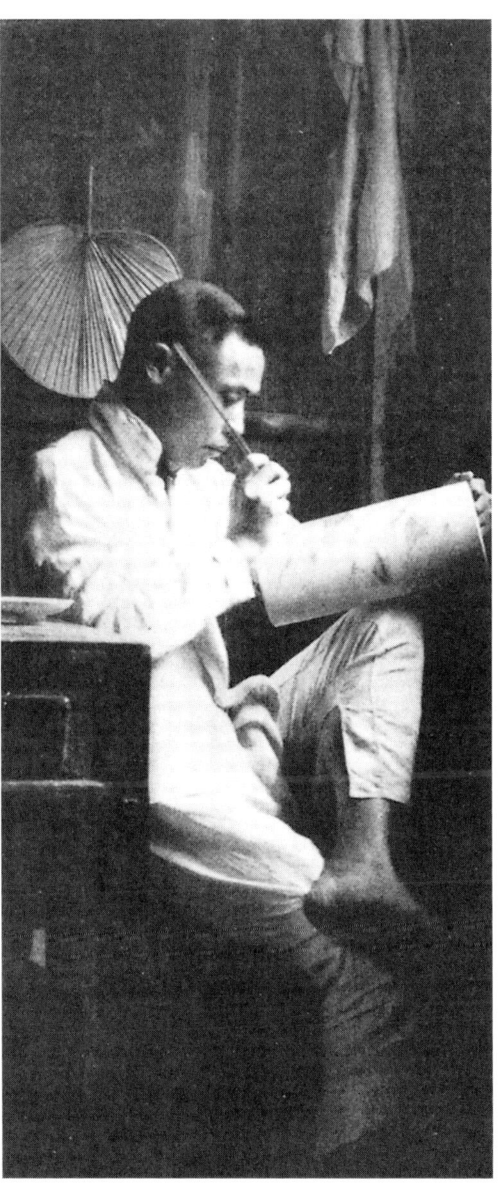

THE BEST DECORATIVE ARTISTS RECEIVE THREE DOLLARS A DAY (MEXICAN)

The unskilled wielders of the brush earn as little as twelve or fifteen cents a day, however. The men are paid not by the hour, but according to the quality of their work and the number of pieces finished.

PORCELAIN HAS BEEN MADE HERE SINCE 220 A.D.

Historically, it dates back to the Han Dynasty, 220 A.D., during which period we find the first records of the production of porcelain in China, though earthenware vessels were probably produced some centuries earlier.

Two main streets, about three miles long and conforming to the contour of the river, comprise the principal thoroughfares.

The city is about a mile wide. Furnaces, warehouses, shops, and homes are crowded together in a hopeless tangle. Great mounds of chipped and defective porcelain, clay chips, and broken dishes are piled high along the river bank. In fact, we first noticed these pieces of porcelain in the bed of the stream several miles below the city, washed down by high water. These dumps must be 30 or 40 feet thick. They represent the accumulated offcastings of the kilns for centuries. From an eminence to the west I counted 78 big yellow chimneys, this number being about half the smokestacks in the city. It is said that Ching-teh-chen in her most flourishing days boasted several thousand kilns.

A CITY OF 300,000 POPULATION WITHOUT A NEWSPAPER

The most unusual feature of the City of Porcelain is its conservatism. "Bu k'ai t'ung" (not open to communications) is heard on every hand. Although China is the home of the printing-press, there is not a single newspaper, either daily or weekly, published in this city of more than a quarter of a million inhabitants. The reason given for this unprogressive state of affairs is that the magistrates have always opposed the press, on the one hand because they are afraid of its political influence, and on the other because of the financial support that would be involved.

ONE METHOD OF APPLYING PORCELAIN GLAZE

Here the operator is blowing the glaze through a bamboo tube as the vase is slowly revolved by his toe.

Ching-teh-chen is devoid of electric lights and telephones. The few rickshaws which now facilitate communications are fighting for existence. While we were in the city a number of workingmen's guilds petitioned the Chamber of Commerce to abolish the rickshaws on the ground that they interfered with traffic.

There are many indications of progress, however. Christianity is influencing the life of the city through three Protestant churches—the China Inland Mission, the Methodist Episcopal, and the American Protestant Episcopal—and the Catholic Church, which has been in Ching-teh-chen for 60 years.

A park, located beside a lotus-covered lake, is the recent creation of a liberal-minded magistrate. Within two years this has developed into a social center, with its industrial museum, restaurant arbors, open paths, and walks. It is the only place in the city where one can get a breath of fresh air.

The Orphan Asylum is an institution that cannot be overlooked. It should be properly named the Abandoned Girl Baby Asylum. Last

MAKING THE FAMOUS RICE-PATTERN WARE

Patient skill and no small amount of time are required in making this pattern, which is known in Ching-teh-chen as "ling lung." It is made not by pressing kernels of the grain into the wet clay, but by cutting the apertures with a sharp knife, after which the holes are filled by repeated dipping into the glazing fluid (see text, page 74).

year 245 girl babies were received by this institution through a small door in a revolving barrel which is located in a niche near the front gate. Later these babies were sent out into the homes of the city to become wives and servants of the well-to-do class.

A DOZEN EXCELLENT CLAYS FOUND NEAR THE CITY

Ching-teh-chen has twenty-two schools enrolling about 2,000 pupils of grammar-grade age. The Chamber of Commerce is a live organization, housed in a modern foreign-style building and headed by a merchant-scholar of much executive ability.

The geographical location of Ching-teh-chen is not accidental. It became the pottery center of the country centuries ago because of the enormous quantities of excellent clay in the district around Po Yang Lake. More than a dozen kinds of excellent clay are found in the neighborhood of the lake.

The chief places from which the hard paste comes are Nan K'an, Yu Kan, Tung Keng, and C'hi Men. At C'hi Men, which is just across the border in Anhwei Province, there is a whole mountain of fine white clay.

WHERE THE TEAPOT MULTIPLIES: CHING-TEH-CHEN

In the center of the porcelain industry the product is classified according to shape, as follows: "yuan c'hi," "tso c'hi," and "tiao hsiang"—round ware (cups, bowls, saucers, and plates), irregular rounds (teapots, vases, etc.), and irregulars (statues, trees, etc.). The factories are likewise classified according to the shape of the ware they manufacture.

Two very descriptive words are used by the Chinese in referring to the composition of porcelain—"c'hi ku," or porcelain bone, and "c'hi ro," or porcelain flesh. The former gives strength and brittleness to a vase or bowl, while the latter adds resiliency and toughness. Unless these clays are mixed in the right proportions, the vessels will either sag or crack when placed in the furnace.

Technically, the "bone" clay is kaolin, or China clay. It is an infusible substance derived from decomposed feldspar or granite. The "flesh" clay is a white, fusible material formed from a mixture of feldspar and quartz.

HOW THE POTTER'S WHEEL IS OPERATED

All of these clays are hauled to Ching-teh-chen in the form of soft, white bricks by small, flat-bottomed boats. Thousands of Chinese boatmen are engaged in this work.

After the clays are thoroughly cleansed, sifted, and refined they are kneaded together in varying proportions, usually by a bare-footed boy, until they are ready for the potter. The wet lump of clay is then placed on the knob of the potter's wheel (see page 64).

A POTTER AND HIS UNFINISHED WARE

Almost large enough to have served as the jars in which Ali Baba's Forty Thieves concealed themselves! Those jars of "Arabian Nights" fame might have been made in Ching-teh-chen, for China's ancient porcelain center was manufacturing such wares as early as 220 A. D.

CHEAP PORCELAIN PILED HIGH
ALONG PORCELAIN STREET

The potter's wheel, which was invented by the Chinese, is a huge circular machine, about four feet in diameter, made of heavy timbers to lend it momentum. It rests on a perpendicular axis in a slight depression, or pit, into which water and debris rapidly drain.

The potter is perched above the wheel, with one foot on either side, in order to allow sufficient space for the movement of his hands.

After revolving the wheel swiftly with a short pole, he deftly and with mechanical precision fashions a plate, bowl, or vase. After years of practice he can estimate to within a hair's breadth the proper size.

The piece is then removed and placed on a long tray in front of the potter, where it awaits the next artisan. Handles and other decorations, made in molds, are added, and then the whole is scraped smooth and allowed to dry until it is ready for the next process—the under-glaze decoration.

Several basic colors, like blue and red, can be painted on under the glaze. The glaze is next applied in various ways—by dipping, by blowing on with a tube, or by sprinkling. After the mark has been added the piece is ready for the furnace.

STRAW AND WOOD SCARCE; COAL NOT SUITED FOR KILNS

Porcelain placed in the kiln to be fired has to be protected in strong, cylindrical clay vessels, called saggers. These trays can be used from three to six times before they are ready for the scrap heap on the river bank. Every piece of porcelain, as it is set into the sagger, is placed on a small, round, clay chip, sprinkled with straw ashes. This prevents the fusing together of the two pieces.

The fuel for the furnaces at Ching-teh-chen is of two kinds—straw and wood. Coal has been tried, but it was found that its fumes discolored the porcelain, and accordingly its use was discontinued. Straw is used to burn only the coarser ware.

The fuel problem is a very acute one and it is only with greatest difficulty that wood can be secured at all. The neighboring hills have long ago been deforested, and firewood must be transported to Ching-teh-chen in river boats, often from sources 200 or 300 miles distant. Boats piled high with straw, projecting over the sides almost to the capsizing point, are common sights all along the river. Wood-boats, too, are seen everywhere.

The kilns are large, egg-shaped ovens of brownish brick, fifty feet long and twelve feet high at the highest point. Because of the intense heat, both the kilns and chimneys must be rebuilt annually.

Every piece of porcelain is placed in the furnace with great precision and arranged according to the temperature which is necessary for its complete firing. Only certain pieces can be placed at the top of the kiln.

The furnace when full is entirely bricked up, and the whole contents are kept at a temperature of 1,600 to 2,000 degrees centigrade, usually for a night and a day, after which the kiln is allowed to cool off, and in due time the porcelain is removed. It has been found that one kiln is large enough to keep nine or ten factories in operation.

This completes the process if no decorations other than the under-glaze paintings are desired, but if more elaborate colorings are used further burnings in a smaller kiln take place. In applying other ornamental designs the artist often spends weeks, or even months, in completing a single piece, as was the case with a beautiful vase portraying the five relationships, which we had the pleasure of inspecting in the leading factory in the city.

PORCELAIN IS CLASSIFIED ACCORDING TO SHAPE

We found porcelain to be classified according to shape, as follows: "yuan c'hi," or round ware, which includes cups, bowls, saucers, and

THE WAY IN WHICH PORCELAIN IS MOVED FROM PLACE TO PLACE

The job of porter in a Ching-teh-chen factory would be hazardous for one not blessed with a steady arm, but the percentage of breakage is small.

plates; "tso c'hi," or irregular rounds, including teapots, vases, and small, flat ink and paint boxes; "tiao hsiang," or irregulars, such as images, statues, representations of trees and other objects.

An interesting feature of the manufacturing process is that the factories are also classified according to the shape of the piece they produce—that is, Mr. Wang makes only round ware, or he may even confine himself to the

PACKING PORCELAIN IN RICE STRAW TO BE SHIPPED TO AMERICA

The firm exporting the largest quantity of porcelain and pottery from Ching-teh-chen is a New York concern. Each piece is carefully packed by hand in rice straw before being packed in large boxes.

manufacture of bowls, while Mr. Li's factory is devoted entirely to the production of teapots.

Clustered around the Fukien Guild Hall, in the eastern part of the city, for example, we found about twenty Fukienese families devoting their entire time to the making of images and statues such as the God of War, Goddess of Mercy, the Three Stars—Happiness, Longevity, and Posterity—and the Gods of Harmony.

There is only one plant in Ching-teh-chen which produces all varieties of porcelain and pottery—the Kiangsi Porcelain Company. It was organized several years ago by a number of prominent stockholders on a modern basis. No foreigners are connected with it in any capacity.

We hear a good deal these days about the inability of Chinese to run their own business firms, but the success of this company, which received the grand prize for the best exhibition of porcelain at the Panama Pacific International Exposition in 1915, seems to indicate that they have some business capacity.

THE IMPERIAL POTTERY'S LONG AND NOBLE HISTORY

Among the four hundred male employees of this concern are one hundred formerly engaged by the Imperial Pottery. In fact, with the downfall of the Ching Dynasty in 1911, the

THE POTTERS' MISTAKES

Great mounds of chipped and defective porcelain and broken dishes are piled high along the river bank at Ching-teh-chen.

Kiangsi Porcelain Company took over practically the entire plant of the famous old factory.

The Imperial Pottery had a long and noble history. It was established in the Sung Dynasty, which lasted from 960 to 1279 A.D. The emperor Chiu Tsung, who founded the dynasty, established the manufactory at Ching-teh-chen, and down through the centuries each succeeding emperor gave it his support and encouragement. It is reported that it was a part of Yuan Shih K'ai's imperial plans to reopen the pottery on his ascendancy to the throne. This is but one of the would-be emperor's dreams that was cut short by his sudden death.

Although the empire no longer exists, porcelain is still used in large quantities by officials in Peking. It was my pleasure on several occasions to meet at feasts President Hsu Hsi Chang's representative, who had been in Ching-teh-chen for several months purchasing special wares to be used as gifts in the capital. We visited the factory which filled his orders and saw there dozens of vases, in every stage of development, later to be presented to foreign ambassadors and Mongol princes.

NO UNEMPLOYMENT IN
THE PORCELAIN CITY

There is no unemployment in Ching-teh-chen. Work is plentiful, but industrial conditions are bad. Long hours, poor food, no rest days, and unsanitary living conditions cause a great deal of dissatisfaction among the laborers.

Workers are organized first according to the parts of the country from which they come—Ching-teh-chen, from Anhwei and all other provinces. They are further formed into guilds, according to the kind of work upon which they are engaged. Strikes are not infrequent, but there is seldom resort to violence. The Chamber of Commerce is a regular mediator.

Many women are engaged in various forms of porcelain production, such as painting, engraving, and lettering. The apprentice system prevails throughout the industry, as in every trade in China. It was interesting to note the artistic ability of a number of small boys engaged in painting birds, flowers, fish, and bats, the last being an omen of good fortune.

Wages range from ten cents to one dollar per day, Mexican, for potters and molders. This includes food and room. The artist's wage ranges from twelve cents to three dollars per day, varying not according to the number of hours, but according to the number and quality of the pieces produced. But no artisan must work too long. If a man is found doing too much and working beyond the time limit, he is set upon by his fellow-workers and severely beaten.

We learned from the revenue collector that about $5,000,000 worth of porcelain and pottery is shipped out of Ching-teh-chen every year. Every piece has to be hauled down the river in small boats to Raochow, whence it is reshipped in large junks to Shanghai and other cities. Most of this is for domestic use, the Chinese not yet having learned the value of stimulating international trade.

"LING LUNG," OR RICE
PATTERN DISHES, REQUIRE
MUCH TIME AND SKILL

Perhaps the most popular design of porcelain with foreigners is the "ling lung," or rice pattern found in dishes, cups and bowls.

The Chinese have learned the art of producing foreign-style dinner sets in this pattern and are finding a ready market for them.

Patient skill and no small amount of time are required for the making of the rice pattern. The wet clay is first formed into a crude cup or plate on the potter's wheel. After the piece has dried for several hours or for a day, it is carefully scraped with a special kind of knife which conforms to the curvature of the vessel. The next step is to cut in the kernel-shaped holes. This is done by a skilled workman, who uses a small, flexible steel lancet.

I had always thought that the rice pattern was made by pressing kernels of rice into the damp clay. It was not until I saw the actual process that this erroneous impression was corrected. After these small apertures have been completed the vessel is ready for the under-glaze painting. Decorating finished, the next step is to apply the glazing fluid. This is a thin, milky substance of high-grade porcelain. Sometimes the bowl is dipped, but the cold, raw liquid is usually put on with a soft wool brush.

The operation is repeated about thirty times, with an interval for drying, until all the holes are filled. Five or six coatings only can be applied in one day. The piece is then fired in the usual manner, and comes out of the furnace with the filled holes standing out in beautiful translucent designs.

The firm exporting the largest quantity of porcelain from Ching-teh-chen is a Chinese company in New York City.

Each piece is carefully packed by hand in rice straw before it is packed in large boxes. These foreign boxes are made in Ching-teh-chen, and after being marked both in Chinese and English are shipped directly to New York.

CHING-TEH-CHEN
HAS A BIG FUTURE

The outstanding impression which a Westerner carries away from this teeming industrial city is the primitiveness of the methods in use.

In not a single shop or factory does one find modern machines. Not even the simplest mechanical devices for operating a series of wheels by means of belts are to be found. Every piece of porcelain is turned out by hand—or by foot.

Yet it is astonishing how much these patient workmen produce with their obsolete methods and crude devices. New ideas penetrate interior China slowly, but with the opening of the Nanking-Nanchang Railway, which has been planned and surveyed, Ching-teh-chen will assume a position of commercial influence that will astonish the world. The enormous clay deposits, together with the quantity of cheap labor, touched by the magic hand of a twentieth-century artist-engineer will push this old and interesting city into a position that will far outshine her ancient glory.

"THE MAN IN THE STREET" IN CHINA

Some Characteristics of the Greatest Undeveloped Market in the World of Today

By Guy Magee, Jr.

CHINA offers today more allurements, both to the legitimate promoter and to the professional exploiter, than any other quarter of the globe. With four hundred million people, a market of tremendous potentiality already established; cheap, intelligent labor abundant; money worshiped, and a national spirit yet lacking—what could present a more inviting field for enterprise?

So much misinformation, or rather lack of information, is extant in regard to the everyday characteristics of this great people that the present seems opportune to acquaint ourselves with the "man in the street." In numbers he is second only to the agricultural class; in importance as a market for immediate foreign development he stands first.

In forming our opinions of things Oriental, either from a cultural or a commercial point of view, care should be taken in the selection of an informant.

THEY DO NOT "ALL LOOK ALIKE"

Beware of the much-traveled acquaintance who, upon being asked what the Chinese or Japanese look like at home, tells us that "they all look alike" to him. His information does not extend beyond the resident foreigners, hotels, and steamers concerning which he always is ready to deluge us with a description applicable to any part of the globe.

A real man of affairs returning from the Orient would not refer to the Chinese or Japanese as "all looking alike" to him; he knows better; also, it is not politic. The Orientals resent having this phrase applied to them, feeling it more as a cultural than as a physical slight, an insult to their civilization and its antiquity, of which they are justly proud.

Furthermore, because of their diverse occupations and intellectual attainments, they feel themselves differentiated from one another;

A CHINESE TOY MERCHANT PEDDLING HIS WARES IN THE STREET

Toys of the same sort that delight youngsters of the Western World gladden the hearts of Chinese children. In the bazaars of Peking the shopper finds flutes and drums, tops, diminutive sets of furniture and dishes for dolls, jointed bamboo dragons, tufted camels, and gaudy tigers of painted canvas stuffed with sawdust (see "The City of the Unexpected," page 15).

hence the added offense in grouping them at random.

Our Oriental friends, particularly the Chinese, have a physical and cultural individuality comparable with that of any other nation, albeit developed under a different civilization.

FOUR DISTINCT TYPES OF CHINESE

In China the variations of type from north to south are so marked that they might be likened to well-defined strata in a sedimentary geological formation having a slight disturbance

THE MAN IN THE STREET IN CHINA IS APT TO BE
A GENIAL INDIVIDUAL, IF PROPERLY APPROACHED

These men are employees of the Shanghai-Nanking Railroad, and their work has brought them in contact with foreigners, so they are no longer shy in the presence of Western travelers.

in the central layers, the disturbance representing a social upheaval in the Yangtze Valley. Upon close examination each stratum resolves itself into numerous less clearly defined secondary strata; in like manner the east and west racial belts are made up of numerous weakly defined groups.

In coastal or mid-China, omitting the west or highlands, the following four distinct types or strata stand out between Manchuria on the north and Cochin China on the south, or very roughly between Peking and Hongkong:

1. North of the Yellow River the Manchus predominate. They are a tall, large-boned, stolid type.

2. South of the Yellow River, but within its basin, there has been sufficient admixture of the original Chinese element to modify somewhat the Manchu characteristics. This type is not so tall, large-boned, or stolid as its northern neighbor. Their faces are often more expressive.

3. South of the Yellow River basin is the Yangtze Valley, which up to the middle of the nineteenth century contained a type, a distinct mean between the northern Manchu and the southern Chinese. The social upheaval caused by the Taipings unstabilized the existing blend and a new one is being evolved, medium in stature and inclining to the south in facial characteristics.

HERE THE PHOTOGRAPHER HAS CAPITALIZED THE NATIVE CURIOSITY OF
CHILDREN, WHICH OUTWEIGHS INSTINCTIVE DISLIKE FOR THE FOREIGNER

The boy in the foreground is the son of a well-to-do tradesman of the Yangtze Valley. The features of the boy wearing the foreign cap are suggestive of the southern type. The child to the right and rear of the boy is a slave girl (see text, page 85).

4. South of the Yangtze Valley are the native Chinese, as distinguished from the Manchu or mixed races, culminating in their marked characteristics in the Cantonese. They have a slight, rather graceful stature, and intelligent and mobile features.

THE YANGTZE VALLEY CHINESE ARE BEST KNOWN TO TRAVELERS

The type occupying the Yangtze Valley is the largest, the most accessible, and probably the best known to the foreigner. In this large group there is far less homogeneity than in any one of the other three, and, generally speaking, this rather curious fact may be traced to two entirely different causes—one natural, the other artificial.

The natural cause is the intermarriage for nearly 400 years of the northern, or Manchu, type with the southern, or Chinese. The artificial cause is the great Taiping Rebellion; it was of far-reaching effect, and is more noticeable in its traces today, although only seventy years have passed, than the earlier intermingling of Manchus and Chinese.

The extent of the social upheaval caused by the Taipings may be partially grasped when it is considered that the best historians, native as well as foreign, concede that, fire and famine assisting, more than forty million people perished in the rebellion.

THE YOUTHFUL ACROBAT ALWAYS ATTRACTS A GROUP OF INTERESTED
SPECTATORS WHEN HE GIVES HIS OUTDOOR PERFORMANCE IN A CHINESE CITY

The agile entertainer works with an extremely simple outfit—a trestle, a tea-cup, and a peg for his jacket. Here he has chosen the station platform for his stage and the hour of his performance is just before train time, when the crowd cannot melt away as the "hat is passed."

To remove any doubt regarding these figures one has only to visit some of the larger native cities—Soochow, Nanking, and Hangchau, for example—and see the large intramural areas to this day razed and unpopulated: then consider that the same devastation extends hundreds of miles along the broad sweep of the valley, and that millions of the slain were replaced by the invaders.

In general, the march of the rebels was from west to east down the valley of the Yangtze, dispersing myriads of families and thousands of communities; some of the people fled north, some south, and some in the van of the invasion.

Upon reaching the sea, progress was checked; pursuers and pursued recoiled upon each other in a great struggling mass. A retrograde movement to the west set in, but, lacking organization and objective, it soon spent itself.

As motion ceased, the flotsam and jetsam settled in its tracks and intermarried not only with its own, but also with the remnants of its precursors, the aforementioned admixture of north and south. Manchu conqueror and conquered Chinese.

Today the inhabitants of the lower reaches of the Yangtze basin are largely an average of all the former types between Siberia and Cochin China and east of the Himalayas. Strange to say, this complex blend of several widely differing components does not vary greatly from the type of the days before the rebellion.

THE TYPICAL "MAN IN THE STREET"

The accompanying illustrations are typical of "the man in the street" of the larger cities in the Yangtze Valley.

Adult Chinese, particularly women, are shy and superstitious, and greatly resent being photographed; even a liberal "cumshaw" often fails to secure the good will of a desirable study. Happily, where money fails strategy sometimes succeeds. By facing at right angles to the objective, suspicion is allayed, and in the case of a folding camera, location in the finder is no more difficult. Several of the photographs reproduced in this article were so taken; for example, that on page 79, in which the children are staring straight into the camera while being photographed unwittingly.

The illustration on page 78, from a photograph taken near Soochow, the provincial capital, some eighty miles from Shanghai, shows two employees of the Shanghai-Nanking Railroad. This picture is included as evidence that our Chinese neighbors can laugh and even

appear genial, contrary to the reports of some returned travelers and in spite of the fact that the other views fail to bring this out. The reason is not far to seek: the railway hands are accustomed to the foreigner and his ways; the others are not.

Lack of self-consciousness is a Chinese characteristic. And yet this statement is relative. The upbringing of the Oriental and that of his neighbors is identical and has been standardized for centuries. Consequently in his own familiar environment from day to day there is nothing to startle him; all that life has to offer he has experienced. But were he forced unexpectedly to don Western clothes, including morning coat and silk hat, and set about his duties, his discomfiture would be just as great as would be ours attending to our affairs in coolie garb.

Changing social conditions sometimes catch us unawares. In the Orient such an occurrence heretofore has been unknown. In peering below the surface it is seen that generalizations between Orient and Occident are mostly superficial, and the differences, being more apparent than real, disappear with fuller understanding of the East. It is a truism that "human nature is much the same the world over."

THE CHINESE ARE BOULEVARDIERS

In large measure the Chinese are as much boulevardiers as the Parisians; in fact, they outvie the Parisians by having their entire meal in full view of the passing crowds. Of the faces turned our way in the illustration on page 92 even the most casual tourist would hardly term them so deficient in individuality as to "all look alike" to him.

The stolidness of these several expressions would suggest a Manchu strain; the physiques

"WHERE THE PARENTS CAN AFFORD IT, CHINESE CHILDREN ARE WELL NURTURED"

suggest the racial mixture of the Yangtze Valley. The apparel is not different from that of clerks and coolies employed in small shops.

Notice the frowns here as compared with the smiles of our railroad employees. "The intrusion is resented, but being powerless to prevent it, we will, with bad grace, submit"; so we interpret the thought behind the expressions in this and in several other illustrations— ungracious but not dangerous; the ill will of unfamiliarity.

Of the two coolies shown in the illustration on page 83 the one to the right, in his well-worn attire, is remotely suggestive of a pre-war Macedonian brigand. His companion has struck an attitude, particularly with the limbs, which would not be without grace were the lines more evident. However, being of a practical rather than of an esthetic turn of mind, he prefers his nether parts to be draped in winter.

The occupations of the two men are indicated by the woven straps terminating in loops passing around the neck; they are wheelbarrow coolies, and daily perform feats of strength, endurance, and clever balancing to imitate

THE STRAPS OVER THE SHOULDERS OF THESE STURDY MEN
PROCLAIM THEIR OCCUPATION—WHEELBARROW COOLIES

The careless or unskillful not infrequently sustain painful bruises and broken ribs when their heavily laden vehicles capsize (see text, page 85). The brawn of the wheelbarrow coolie has reduced the cost of moving package freight to an unheard-of minimum, and thereby contributed largely to the prosperity of the treaty ports.

which it would take a Westerner months, even years, to learn.

Pushing a wheelbarrow in China is a dangerous occupation, many a broken rib and back resulting therefrom. This is so contrary to our own experience that to understand it we must have a conception of how a native wheelbarrow is constructed and handled, a high degree of specialization being involved in each.

The construction is somewhat as follows: the wheel, nearly a yard in diameter, is shod with a heavy, grooved tire to prevent skidding, an ever-present danger, and is placed centrally between two slatted platforms, each about

HE TELLS YOUR FORTUNE, BUT HE IS THINKING
MORE OF HIS FEE THAN OF THINGS OCCULT

The soothsayer is a popular "institution" in China. His services are invoked to set propitious days for weddings, funerals, and burials. In this land of contradictions, the funeral and the burial seldom, if ever, take place together, and the soothsayer is the individual who causes and profits by the delay (see text, page 90).

three feet long and a foot wide, carried on a framework. some inches above the axle. Part of the frame extends beyond the platform, ending in two strong handles; below is the usual pair of legs.

Operation of the barrow is somewhat complicated. Assume a load of cotton, one most difficult to manage. Two bales, *half a ton*, are securely roped onto the parallel platform. The coolie then enters the shafts, or handles, first slipping over them the loops of his strap, which is of such length that, with his shoulders straightened, the legs of the barrow clear the ground.

The handles are grasped with *palms down*, for, remember, the shoulders carry the unbalanced load; the arms, assisted by the weight of the body, are exerted only in controlling the balance. The balance also may be accomplished by raising and lowering the shoulders and planting the feet firmly—a sort of emergency measure requiring a halt, and therefore seldom used, for every coolie knows that time out is money out.

The danger lies in having an upset, which frequently occurs through skidding; hence the heavy, grooved tire. Collisions, too, are common, as generally the coolie cannot see over his load.

When a load of baled cotton upsets it rolls over, so that the wheelbarrow takes a position upside down, and unless the coolie quickly slips out of his strap and backs clear of the handles, the latter, in revolving, will pin him to the ground, one above, one below his body suggestive of being broken on the wheel and probably no more agreeable.

THE COOLIE WEARS OUT QUICKLY

The continual physical strain while at work ages these coolies very rapidly. The two shown on page 83, being comparatively young, do not reveal the effects so plainly as would their fellows several years older. After twenty-five the wear and tear is evident.

Frequently, owing to unbalanced loading, as when only one bale is carried, the barrow must be tilted to maintain equilibrium. Five hundred pounds, balanced on one side of a wheel, shoved along amid the distractions of a narrow, crowded street—no wonder that the strain reacts on the expression!

Owing to the demands of the work, wheelbarrow coolies are generally recruited from a locality near Chin Kiang on the Yangtze River, where the people, largely of Manchu stock, suffered little dispersion in the Taiping Rebellion. They are larger and stronger than their neighbors.

The wheelbarrow coolie's song has yet to be sung, though many an undeserved word of opprobrium has been hurled at him. Native and foreigner alike abuse him for blocking the traffic with his snail-like pace and enormous load, yet he looms large as an economic factor. Under certain conditions he has reduced the cost of moving package freight to an unheard-of minimum, and thereby his lowly efforts have contributed largely to the wonderful prosperity of the treaty ports and especially to that of Shanghai.

Possibly in the distant future he, with his faithful vehicle, will be remembered in bronze and stone as a pillar supporting Commerce.

In the illustration on page 79, accident brought together a greater variety of features than long search and studied arrangement could have done. In the child, native curiosity has outweighed the instinctive dislike for the foreigner; the photographer was so hemmed in that he scarcely had room to manipulate his camera.

A GLANCE AT THE CHILDREN

The little boy, with bulging cheeks and pug nose, occupying the greater part of the foreground, is typical of the sons of well-to-do tradesmen in hundreds of the Yangtze Valley cities. Where the parents can afford it, Chinese children are well nurtured. They also have a predisposition to chubbiness—a happy condition for the children, but provoking to the ethnologist to be baffled by a chubbiness common alike to north, south, and middle China.

A REPAIRER OF "RICKSHAW" COVERS PLYING HIS TRADE

As "the child is father to the man," the man in his case gives promise of being large-boned and full-bodied.

The little chap to the left, wearing a foreign cap, might be a brother of the chubby boy, own or half, or as the Chinese subtly put it, having in mind plural marriage, "same mother" or "same father." His features, except for the thick under-lip, are more suggestive of the southern type in childhood.

The three others on the extreme left show individuality, if not character. They will serve as

CAUGHT SEWING IN A SUNNY ANGLE OF HER WALL

well as any other three to represent the "young man in the street"—household servants, clerks, coolies for light work, artisans, etc. Although receiving but scant notice, he is the backbone of his class and of prime importance to the foreigner of commerce.

The face to the right and rear of the chubby boy, the one standing out so distinctly is of the so-called slave girl.

Probably born on a small boat, of parents with no land abode, this unfortunate, to provide room or more food for a favored son, was spared drowning only to be sold into slavery. The drawn features in one so young and the dumbfounded expression attest a childhood of want and ill treatment, an overworked and undernourished body.

Occasionally these little slaves are accorded better treatment, but, to China's disgrace, such is the exception rather than the rule. To speculate upon racial strains in a body and features so distorted by "man's inhumanity to man" is futile.

WOMEN AN ECONOMIC ENCUMBRANCE IN CHINA

The density of population in China has for centuries brought home to the people a knowledge that "survival of the fittest" is more than a theory, that it is a stern reality. In the struggle for existence the superfluous female members of the family are felt to be an encumbrance; hence it is purely from an economic point of view that girls are regarded by the lower classes with disfavor bordering on hostility.

According to the Chinese social system, a daughter and son, as family assets, have no basis of comparison; at the same time there is no animosity toward the female just because there happens to be a distinction called sex. However, it does not help the poor little slave's hard lot to know herself to be the victim of oppressive economic conditions that have warped the better nature of her persecutors.

The coarse, protruding, thick-lipped mouth so clearly shown behind the little slave girl, also evident in the latter and in the coolie in the center, seems to be a mark of privation, acquired or hereditary, frequently seen in the country where famine is current and living conditions are hard.

A NATION OF ACROBATS

Up to the arrival of the motion picture, some six years ago, the Chinese, even in the larger cities, had little in the way of really stimulating amusement. Their theater is devoted to constant repetition of classic dramas, acted and costumed in accordance with traditions and conventions centuries old, so that by contrast our small street entertainer, shown on page 80, is always sure of an audience glad to welcome a bit of novelty.

The agility, small feet, and shapely hands show a southern ancestry, although the features savor more of the mixed Yangtze type. In this case our inference may be wrong; he may be a chubby-faced Cantonese stroller far from home.

Observe the simplicity of his outfit—a trestle, a tea-cup, and a peg for his jacket. He will entertain the crowd for twenty minutes, perhaps half an hour, and no "fool pidgin," but "straight comedy" all the time. Some vaudeville performers might well take heed.

The selection of a location would do credit to a seasoned fakir. When traveling, the Chinese are well beforehand—hence this performance before train time on the packed station platform, where the crowd, being thick and fenced in, cannot melt away when the hat is passed around. Also, on a "gala occasion" the travelers are supposed to have a little extra change and a liberal feeling withal.

In the south especially, Chinese children are very agile, as witness their game of battledore and shuttlecock, in which the bat is replaced by either foot, striking the *shuttle* with the inside of the instep just below the anklebone. Practice makes them so adept that many returns are made without a miss.

It is games such as these, centuries old, that adapt a people to the easy mastery of acro-

A PERAMBULATING CHINESE RESTAURANT

This restaurateur is prepared to serve a meal wherever he finds a customer. He carries his kitchen and his dining-room equipment at the ends of a long pole, which he balances on his shoulder.

batic feats. Probably the reason so many vaudeville and circus acrobats are Swiss is that as a nation the people have been trained for generations in collective physical exercises.

THE HIGH COST OF DYING IN CHINA

Idle curiosity sometimes beguiles us into reading a patent-medicine advertisement, so it might lead us into having our fortune told by the old gentleman shown on page 84. However, provided we tender sound silver in return, he is not concerned with our reason for consulting him. Superstition is so ingrained in the Chinese people that its imprint appears in their faces.

Days for weddings, funerals, and burials are named by a soothsayer. In the case of burials it

CHINESE WOMEN GREATLY RESENT BEING PHOTOGRAPHED

Girls are regarded with disfavor by the lower classes in China purely from an economic point of view. In the struggle for existence, the superfluous females of the family are felt to be an encumbrance.

might frequently be worth while to employ a second diviner to report on the veracity of the first; for, until the burial finally takes place, the soothsayer makes reports, for a consideration each time, on the progress of his divinations until, the patience of the family finally becoming exhausted, a day is speedily decided upon and the body laid away, generally in a family plot in the country.

In this land of contradictions, the funeral and burial seldom, if ever, occur together. In the case of the average tradesman the funeral removes the body as far as the "mortuary," a large one-story building or group of buildings, on the outskirts of the city, in which space is rented for temporarily depositing the coffin until the heavens, interpreted by the diviner, indicate the advent of a suitable day for interment.

At Canton this above-ground purgatory is so crowded that there is always a "line" exposed to the weather waiting to get in. Such a city of the dead might seem unhygienic in a subtropical climate until it is considered that their big coffins permit the use of a thick cushion of lime entirely surrounding the body.

It frequently happens that when the home of the deceased is in a distant city the body may be halted several times on its way until the

CHINESE BLACKSMITHS TAKE NO CHANCES WHEN SHOEING HORSES: PEKING

This sling-like arrangement of ropes and knots permits the business in hand to be dispatched with greatest ease and no danger.

soothsayer in each stopping place gives the word for proceeding. What one might term the "overhead" of a well-to-do funeral is considerable.

The services of the fortune-teller are in demand to select a day for commencing a long journey or embarking upon an important financial venture—that is, a big gamble in piece goods or oil stock, blending ancient superstition and modern high finance, and for many other occasions in the daily life of the people—so that the soothsayer, if he has tact and astuteness, need not lack a clientele.

The rather somnolent and introspective expression of our old man—a type in which southern characteristics predominate—is misleading. Instead of being bent upon mysticism, his thoughts are, in conjunction with the corner of his eye, busily engaged in figuring out what will be his "cumshaw" for posing.

THE FAMILY IS THE UNIT

It has been mentioned that the law of the "survival of the fittest" has been known to the Chinese through experience for centuries, and now and then, as one encounters a victim of its working, he is impressed by its inexorable application. In China individualism and nationalism are practically unknown; so that no provision is made by one person for the succor of

THE CHINESE BILL-POSTER KNOWS A GOOD LOCATION WHEN HE
SEES IT, EVEN IF HE HAS TO UTILIZE THE REAR WALL OF A TEMPLE

another. The family is the unit, founded on the principle of mutual assistance.

With such a social system in a land where the struggle for existence is severe, an individual mentally or physically defective to any degree is handicapped at the outset. Sweep away his family, as not infrequently happens overnight, by flood, epidemic, or famine on land, or through storm among the boat population, and his sole salvation is to become deranged. In the picture on page 95 is shown such an unfortunate—a lone piece of humanity, devoid of kith and kin, and unfitted, though by no act of his own, to compete on even terms with the more efficient.

Physical suffering as well as mental anguish have held sway until the mind could no longer stand the strain; all is written on the features; the attitude and expression show entire insensibility to his present lot; in so far he is

fortunate. He is even excluded from fraternizing with the professional beggars, who maintain a highly organized guild.

Though prevalent in every city, this homeless man fortunately is typical of a class few in numbers. The condition of the male is pitiful—too pitiful to invite reflection upon the condition of the female. His misfortune is common to both north and south, Manchu and Chinese, and all crosses and mixtures.

TWO CLASSES OF OCCUPATIONS— CREATIVE AND NON-CREATIVE

Many causes are responsible for China's impotence while harboring the greatest potentiality of any nation, both in man-power and in physical opportunity. These causes are not far to seek; some are self-evident.

LIKE THE PARISIANS, THE CHINESE FREQUENTLY
TAKE THEIR MEALS IN VIEW OF THE PASSING CROWDS

The stolidness of their expressions suggests a Manchu strain, while the physiques of the diners in public are indicative of the racial mixture to be found in the Yangtze Valley (see text, page 81).

Like most countries, the Chinese social system has many defects; its wonderful endurance, however, is due to its several good qualities. That which has to do with classifying the pursuits of man in the order of their importance to the state is theoretically sound, but too inelastic to meet modern conditions.

All occupations are divided into two classes—creative and non-creative. Other things being equal, the former have decided preference over the latter.

AGRICULTURE STANDS FIRST AMONG THE CREATIVE OCCUPATIONS

First in the list of the creative group stands agriculture. Theoretically, the farmer takes precedence over all others, literati excepted.

Then follow the various trades—cook, carpenter, mason, smith, etc.

On the other side are the military, actors, barbers, police, etc.

For centuries occupation, not wealth, personality, or family, determined the social position; so that the non-creative group, containing many barred from public office, even from the privilege of owning land, in time came to be despised. All who could do so sought other, more respected livelihoods; so that association with a non-creative occupation was looked upon as a sign of mental or physical inferiority.

WHY THE CHINESE POLICEMAN IS WEAK

There probably was a long period in Chinese history in which ethical culture was real and guided men in their daily intercourse to such a degree that organized police were unnecessary. That day has passed, but the social system adapted to such an ideal state does not admit it; hence, to maintain law and order, to cope with evil-doers mentally and physically capable, many employed as policemen are mentally and physically unfit. In a group on the street in a treaty port it not infrequently happens that the weakest physique belongs to the policeman.

In the "closed" cities the police force is in an even more deplorable condition, being scarcely uniformed and having hardly the authority of coolies and no means of enforcing that little.

On the other hand, the Sikh policeman, frequently seen in China on the streets of the foreign concessions, is wonderfully efficient, without being brutal, in his control of the natives. The Sikh suggests efficiency nurtured on law and order; the native policeman suggests inefficiency caused by lack of legal regulation and by a defective social system. The two policemen are typical of the difference between Orient and Occident, the Sikh having had the advantage of British army training.

COMMERCIAL COMPETITION IS ALONG NATIONAL LINES

The trite saying that "commerce knows no flag" does not hold in the Orient, where foreign competition is almost along national lines. To stimulate trade, new legitimate wants should be stimulated.

Only careful study and long residence enable competent commercial agents to introduce new products. A market once gained, however, tends to perpetuate itself; so that initial expenditure is all that need be considered.

Those whose commercial acquaintance is with less industrious peoples should be reminded that there is a vast difference between these and the Chinese, in that the Chinese do not have to be stimulated to work in order to earn the wherewithal to spend; all labor willingly in the "vineyard" and all have something in hand for a rainy day.

The Chinese are always in the market for a bargain and are economical not sentimental, buyers.

UNFAMILIARITY WITH LOCAL CONDITIONS LEADS TO LOSS

Lack of a little local knowledge has frequently led to large commercial loss. Some years ago the electrical equipment for the tramways in a southern Oriental city was ordered from one of our leading companies. After operation commenced it was found that the controllers were too high for the average motorman; his arm quickly tired. This was remedied by each motorman providing himself with a little platform. In the Orient, anything detachable is generally supplied by the user.

The well-informed manufacturer would have prevented the mistake in controller design and have secured a permanent market as well. European competitors were quick to introduce a controller of suitable height, through which they secured this company's subsequent business.

The types of Chinese which have been considered here are those of the street, comparable in the West to those of the small shop districts; officials, literati, and wealthy merchants have not been considered, for a Westerner having opportunity to observe them would be too well versed in native affairs to confess that "all Chinese look alike" to him.

HOMELESS MAN

Devoid of kith and kin, physical suffering and mental anguish have held sway until his mind could no longer endure the strain. When he loses his family, the man in the street in China loses the great stabilizing influence of his life.

A NATIVE OF PEKING ATTIRED FOR COLD WEATHER

The north winds are bitingly cold in Peking, killing vegetation and freezing rivers and lakes. The "Mongolian wind" is a hurricane, which fills the air with such clouds of dust as to make the sun seem in eclipse.

SHIFTING SCENES ON THE STAGE OF NEW CHINA

An understanding of the present condition of unrest and political chaos in China is impossible without some knowledge of the background of the past.

The form of China's government under the empire might be compared to that established by Alexander the Great after his conquest of the world. The Emperor at Peking stood at the head of a country divided into independent provinces ruled by satraps, or governors, whose sole obligation to the central government was completed when they sent to the imperial treasury their allotted quotas of imperial revenue and insured peace within their respective provincial boundaries.

These satraps were the product of and were assisted in their work by the younger and less advanced products of the literary examination system. They composed the mandarinate, or civil-service class, which monopolized the educated element of the nation.

The end and aim of an ambitious young man under this system was to pass successfully the examinations and thereby obtain preferment in the civil administration of the country. There was no need for education in any other walk in life.

Held together at first by a strong alien ruling house which they despised, members of the mandarinate later came to support that house (the Manchus) as the panoply of a government upon which they depended for their station in life.

A SHOCK TO CHINA'S PRIDE

A government may retain the confidence of the people it governs as long as it is maintained in the interests of the governed and not its own employees. It must react promptly to the demands of the governed, both as to domestic well-being and in its relation with outside nations. When this test is applied, the government maintained in its latter days by the mandarinate is found wanting.

Distrust grew, rebellion followed. For years the government had allowed the public works of the country to go unrepaired; nor was money spent on new work.

In 1894 the people suffered a shock to their pride and trust in this government through the defeat of their armies at the hands of the Japanese. The nation, besides losing

OUTSIDE THE WALLS OF PEKING

The coolie a-foot is not carrying a banner with a strange device, his bamboo staff is merely the goad with which he prods the listless donkey of his master.

important territory, was forced to go into the financial markets of the world to borrow money to pay its war indemnities.

The broker nations demanded certain concessions as a *quid pro quo*. There ensued the battle of concessions. Between 1896 and 1898 Russia got Dalny, Germany got Tsingtau, Great Britain got Wei-hai-wei, and France got Kuang-chau-wan.

MANCHUS DIVERTED THE BOXER UPRISING

In 1900 the so-called "Boxer Uprising" occurred, beginning as an attack upon the Manchu Dynasty, which the people blamed for their troubles, internal as well as external.

The Manchu rulers, skillfully diverted the wrath of the so-called uprising from themselves to the foreigner, and thus succeeded in obtaining a few years' reprieve, during which time they made a violent effort to retrieve lost ground and win back the confidence and trust of the people they had so grossly misgoverned. They saw the "handwriting on the wall" and inaugurated an attempt to centralize the government by nationalizing railway construction, adding to the prestige of the army by making the Emperor its commander-in-chief, etc.

But it was too late. The plan for railway construction precipitated a conflict between the forces in favor of centralization and those (greatly in the majority) in favor of continuing the old plan, based on the independence of the provinces.

A HUMAN FERRY IN CHINA

Note the extended tongue of the coolie; it does not indicate fatigue, however.

This conflict was characterized by overt acts of hostility, of which those who had been plotting revolution against the Manchu House took advantage.

In 1911 came the short revolution which within three months brought about the formal abdication of the Manchus, who fired a Parthian shot by turning over the government to Yuan Shih-K'ai, a leader of the strongest party in the mandarinate, who had led the imperial armies against the revolutionists.

When the Manchu House was abolished the panoply of government was gone. There were left the mandarinate—the priests of the temple, as it were—and the common people, who in the aggregate made a great, contented mass, peace-loving but uninterested in government, unleavened by the education which had been reserved for the mandarinate, and therefore unpatriotic.

The mandarinate class was composed of the scholars of the old educational system. The new generation was bringing with it a new set of scholars, for the most part educated abroad, who were returning to China with a profound respect for Western learning and an equally profound contempt for everything for which their fathers stood.

YOUNGER GENERATION INSPIRED REVOLUTION

It was the younger generation that had inspired and helped to organize the successful revolution; but the Manchus had handed the government over to the older generation, the mandarinate, which at once was forced to commence the struggle for very existence against the attacks of the impatient younger generation, dissatisfied with an empty victory.

Thus we find the situation in 1912:

1. The reigning family was gone.

2. Two parties were left struggling to control the government that was to take its place—first, the mandarinate (strongly of the belief that the monarchical form of government was the only one suited to the Chinese), and, second, the new generation of scholars (decidedly imbued with the idea that a democratic form of government modeled upon the plan of the American Republic was not only suited to the Chinese, but to the advanced times in which we live).

And so there resulted the two attempts of the mandarinate to establish a monarchy: First, Yuan Shih-K'ai's attempt to form a dynasty in 1916; next, Chang Hsun's attempt to restore the Manchus.

In the meantime the common people, the merchants and farmers, were sitting by, observing a strict neutrality, suspicious of both sides and apparently helpless.

To the previously mentioned three classes of people in China, namely, the mandarinate (scholars and gentry), the merchants and farmers, and the younger generation of scholars, who are becoming lawyers, teachers, doctors, and engineers, there must be added a fourth class, which must be considered in China as well as in every other country. Marx called them the laboring proletariat. In China they are called coolies. They are the "hewers of wood and drawers of water." Vast numbers of them found employment as porters, muleteers, river boatmen. It was to them at the end of a day of hard toil that opium came as a blessing, affording relief from the grinding fatigue and utter exhaustion which their ill-nurtured bodies suffered.

THE COOLIES PROFOUNDLY AFFECTED BY NEW CONDITIONS

The coolies had been profoundly affected by conditions. In the first place, opium was taken from them, leaving a dissatisfied lot of men who could no longer use it. There were also a few discontented opium-growers, who had been thrown out of work by the destruction of their one money crop.

Then, too, during the past sixty years there has been a great extension of shipping along the coasts, rivers, and canals of China, and many railways have been built. All of these developments have resulted in the changing of trade lanes—the abandonment of old routes for new ones.

For instance, the old highroad that ran from Canton north through Hunan to Hankow was once alive with porters, muleteers, wheelbarrow and chair coolies. As a trade route, it is now dead; for it is cheaper and quicker to supply the country by steamers from Shanghai. The Grand Canal has been abandoned for the quicker and cheaper avenue of the Tientsin-

Pukow Railway and the steamers that ply the coast between Shanghai and Tientsin.

The old caravan route that began at Tientsin, passed through the Great Wall, and ended at Kiahta, in Siberia, over which furs and tea were exchanged, has been abandoned for the railways of Manchuria and the steamers that ply between Shanghai and Vladivostok.

These changes mean that countless numbers of coolies who formerly found employment in the transportation of freight and passengers over those ancient routes have been thrown upon a country the ordinary food-producing population of which has been growing constantly. They form a floating labor population now preying upon the landed population.

THE BACKGROUND FOR TODAY'S EVENTS

Thus we have our background:

First. The mandarinate (trained in a school which emphasized the administrative side of government, and therefore inheriting no belief in the ability of the people to govern themselves through legislation of their own making) struggling to retain control of the administration, inclined toward the monarchical form of government as the one best suited to their needs and the needs of the people but too jealous of one another to be able to set up a reigning family chosen from among themselves.

Second. A peace-loving, unpatriotic merchant and farmer class, which through the centuries has left matters of government in the hands of the mandarinate and which has therefore not inherited any feeling of civic responsibility or patriotism.

Third. The patriotic scholars of the younger generation, who are impatient to take over the work which they feel that the mandarinate of the old order is unfit to do, imbued with a belief in a democratic form of government modeled upon that of the United States.

Fourth. The coolies, discontented, out of work, unpatriotic, ignorant of government, ready to march and fire a gun for any side that will furnish them food, money, and clothing.

A further complicating factor in the situation is the fact that among the Chinese provincial loyalty has been developed to a very high degree, thus injecting into the struggle an element much akin to our old question of "States' Rights."

This is the stage setting for today's political drama.

We are now ready to consider some of the actors.

The mandarinate has always been dominated by strong leaders, similar to our political bosses, who have surrounded themselves by followers (generally fellow-provincials) made loyal through rapid advancement in the civil service of the country.

TWO OPPOSING PARTIES IN THE MANDARINATE

Men rose to leadership through skill in military command or through proved ability as scholars or statesmen. Thus Hunan produced two great military leaders in the persons of Tso, who put down the Mohammedan Rebellion, and Tseng, who helped Li-Hung-Chang put down the Tai-Ping Rebellion. As a result, natives of Hunan dominated the mandarinate for many years. Li-Hung-Chang was himself a native of Anhwei Province and he helped greatly its prestige.

The mandarinate is at present divided into two opposing parties—the Kuang-tung faction, which has had the sympathies and support of the newer generation of scholars, and the Pei Yang Party, led by the followers and protégés of Li-Hung-Chang and Yuan Shih-K'ai. Canton is the center of the former party, Peking of the latter. The Pei Yang was by far the most powerful of the mandarin factions, but it has become divided into cliques during the last few years.

Of these cliques one of the most important was the league of governors of the Yangtze Province, who have maintained a kind of neutrality in the struggle, believing in compromise rather than force as a means of settling the people's differences. Then there were the extremists, like Tuan-Ch'i-jui, who believed in force. Tuan was instrumental in organizing the now famous Anfu Club, composed of the elements in favor of force.

The name Anfu is made up of the first syllables of the names of the Province An(hwei) and Fu(kien), and is therefore supposed to be a union of the forces controlling the Chinese army (Anhwei) and navy (Fukien)—an idea similar to that of the Japanese system, whereby the two clans which have held traditional control over the army (Satsuma) and the navy (Closhu) have combined as the Satcho element to control the Japanese cabinets through those branches of the government administration.

In China the army is by far the more important of the two, and over a thousand of the younger Chinese army officers obtained their education and training in the Japanese army schools.

Until 1914 the issue had been clearly drawn between the mandarinate as a whole and the more modern, radical element. The undivided mandarinate, direct heir to the Manchus, had successfully defended its right to control the administration of the country in 1913 against the attacks of the radicals, led by Sun Yat-sen and others. Loans obtained from Western lending nations assisted them in their control, furnishing them with the financial aid needed in reorganizing the revenues and currency of the country.

During this period Japan, having no money to lend, was thought by the mandarinate to be furnishing refuge and encouragement to the radical element, which was continuously plotting revolt against the party in power; but with the beginning of the World War a new situation was brought about. Europe needed its money, and as a result the mandarinate began to suffer through lack of funds. The radicals began to regain hope.

THE MONARCHICAL FIASCO

In 1916 came the great monarchical fiasco of Yuan Shih-K'ai and the latter's death, some say from a broken heart. He left the government treasury impoverished and the people of the country thoroughly suspicious of the intentions of the mandarinate.

In 1917 America entered the war on the side of the Allies and invited the hitherto neutral nations to join her against the Germans. The mandarinate, now led by Tuan-Ch'i-jui, and the so-called Anfu Club saw in this invitation an opportunity to obtain the financial assistance necessary in putting down revolt and making secure its control of the country. The radical element realized the danger and tried to prevent a declaration of war. The latter had the majority of the people with it, for there was much suspicion of a plan for a return of the Manchu House and there was also a genuine fear that joining the Allies meant throwing China upon the mercy of Japan, already unpopular because of the famous "21 demands" of 1915.

Tuan-Ch'i-jui, who had had his Anfu Club in excellent working trim for some time, by clever tactics obtained his declaration of war,

A QUICK-LUNCH COUNTER IN PEKING

The genial smile of this sidewalk Boniface is a business asset of much account. Note the "steam table" in the foreground and the chef busy over the caldron in the background.

and through the control which the Anfu Club had over the ministries af communications and finance, he was able, on scant security, to get money for his plans from Japanese bankers. He made an attempt to force the radical element in the south to come to terms, but without success.

The close relationship which appeared to exist between his party, the Anfu Club, and Japanese money-lenders gave his enemies in the Pei Yang Party their opportunity. They refused to help him in his efforts to coerce the radicals by military force, bringing about a stalemate and an attempt at a peace conference.

The World War ended with the defeat of Germany, and Japan, faced with a more serious situation in Siberia, cut off the ready supply of funds which was helping the Anfu Party in China. General Wu-Pei-fu, commander of the forces of Chihli Province under Military Governor Ts'ao-K'un—the leader of the Chihli faction of the Pei Yang Party, which was opposed to the Anfu faction—withdrew his troops from between the forces supporting the radicals and those of the Anfu faction, thus precipitating open strife between the two, in which the Anfu faction was defeated.

Tuan-Ch'i-jui, with those loyal to the Anfu Party, attempted to suppress the Chihli faction, but he found that the accumulation of distrust of the mandarinate, himself, and the Anfu Club, the last because of its intrigues with the Japanese, turned the country against him, and he lost.

The alignment in this last struggle was interesting. Dividing the mandarinate of the country as a whole into two factions, we had in the south the Kuang-tung Party, while in the extreme north was the Pei Yang Party, with the neutral league in Central China benevolently neutral toward the extreme north.

In the beginning the new generation of scholars, led by Sun Yat-sen, Tang Shao-yi, and Wu Ting-fang, sided with the Kuang-tung Party and participated in the government which it set up at Canton.

In the spring of 1920 it was evident that there had been a split, however. Sun Yat-sen, T'ang Shao-yi, and Wu Ting-fang severed their connections with the Kuang-tung faction and took with them one of their military leaders, Tang Chi-yao. As already indicated, there had been a split in the Pei Yang Party, between the Chihli faction and the Anfu faction.

THE MANDARINATE STILL IN CONTROL

When the final struggle against Tuan Ch'i-jui came there were not lacking evidences of a joining of forces among T'ang Chi-yao (of the Kuang-tung faction), the leaders of the new generation (Sun Yat-sen, Wu Ting-fang, Tang shao-yi), and the Anfu clique, against which formerly they had been violently opposed.

An understanding seems also to have been reached between the main section of the Kuang-tung faction and the Chihli faction. This latter combination was not only the more natural of the two, based as it was upon the common interests of the two factions of the mandarinate for self-preservation, but it was the more powerful, as it drew to its banner all of the neutral elements, such as the Yangtze league of governors and Chang Tso-lin, military governor of Manchuria. In a few days it had forced Tuan Ch'i-jui to yield his power and give up his soldiers. The Anfu Club was abolished and its members dispersed.

The situation has not changed materially during the last few months. It has been proved that even in China an element cannot survive long on alien support, as the Anfu clique tried to do. The party in control is still the mandarinate, and there is still an opposition, composed of a new generation of students and young men.

FURTHER READING

Jonathan D. Spence's *The Search for Modern China* (1990) is a highly engaging and well-researched piece of scholarship by a renowned expert of Chinese history. See also Robert F. Baldwin and Ray Webb, *Daily Life in Ancient and Modern China* (1999); Patricia Buckley Ebrey, *Cambridge Illustrated History of China* (1996); Stephen G. Haw, *A Traveller's History of China* (1995); Jane Shute, *The Ancient Chinese* (1998).

INDEX

CONTRIBUTORS

General Editor FRED L. ISRAEL is an award-winning historian. He received the Scribe's Award from the American Bar Association for his work on the Chelsea House series *The Justices of the United States Supreme Court*. A specialist in American history, he was general editor for Chelsea's *1897 Sears Roebuck Catalog*. Dr. Israel has also worked in association with Arthur M. Schlesinger, jr. on many projects, including *The History of the U.S. Presidential Elections* and *The History of U.S. Political Parties*. He is senior consulting editor on the Chelsea House series *Looking into the Past: People, Places, and Customs*, which examines past traditions, customs, and cultures of various nations.

Senior Consulting Editor ARTHUR M. SCHLESINGER, JR. is the pre-eminent American historian of our time. He won the Pulitzer Prize for his book *The Age of Jackson* (1945), and again for *A Thousand Days* (1965). This chronicle of the Kennedy Administration also won a National Book Award. He has written many other books, including a multi-volume series, *The Age of Roosevelt*. Professor Schlesinger is the Albert Schweitzer Professor of the Humanities at the City University of New York, and has been involved in several other Chelsea House projects, including the *American Statesmen* series of biographies on the most prominent figures of early American history.